Challenging Common Core Language Arts Lessons

ADVANCED CURRICULUM FROM THE
CENTER FOR GIFTED EDUCATION AT WILLIAM & MARY

Challenging Common Core Language Arts Lessons

Activities and Extensions for Gifted and Advanced Learners in GRADE 4

LINDSAY KASTEN

William & Mary
School of Education
CENTER FOR GIFTED EDUCATION

P.O. Box 8795
Williamsburg, VA 23187

Copyright ©2016 Center for Gifted Education, William & Mary

Edited by Katy McDowall

Cover design by Raquel Trevino and layout design by Allegra Denbo

ISBN-13: 978-1-61821-550-5

Prufrock Press Inc.
P.O. Box 8813
Waco, TX 76714-8813
Phone: (800) 998-2208
Fax: (800) 240-0333
http://www.prufrock.com

TABLE OF CONTENTS

INTRODUCTION

The Common Core State Standards (CCSS) for English Language Arts (ELA) are K–12 curriculum standards that describe the English language arts (ELA) skills and concepts students need to develop for success in higher education and the 21st-century workplace.

The College and Career Readiness Anchor Standards are the basis of the ELA/literacy standards. They specify the core knowledge and skills needed, while grade-specific standards provide specificity. The ELA standards also establish guidelines for literacy in history/social studies, science, and technical subjects for grades 6–12.

With the adoption of the CCSS in nearly every state, gifted and advanced learners need opportunities to master grade-level standards and ELA skills and concepts with greater depth, rigor, and understanding. This book is one of a series of books developed in conjunction with the Center for Gifted Education at William & Mary intended to give gifted and advanced learners additional practice and activities to master and engage with the CCSS for ELA. Each book in the series is organized by the content standards in one grade.

The lessons in this book cover grade 4 ELA content. In grade 4, the standards are addressed in five domains:

- Reading Literature and Informational Text,
- Foundational Skills,
- Language,
- Speaking and Listening, and
- Writing.

PURPOSE

The lessons in this book were written with the assumption that a teacher has already introduced ELA content standards through primary curriculum sources. Reading, writing, and speaking activities enrich and extend current grade-level ELA content rather than accelerate students to above-grade-level content. Each lesson focuses on multiple content standards, due to the overlap of skills inherent in ELA activities, and provides additional support and enrichment for gifted and advanced learners.

BOOK AND LESSON STRUCTURE

This book is divided into four units, each of which contains multiple lessons. Each unit focuses on a theme and centers on the ideas related to the theme within literature and nonfiction texts. Within each unit, students will read, analyze, evaluate, and interpret poetry, short stories, and novels containing the theme. Students will demonstrate their growing understanding of the theme through various projects, narrative writing, informational writing, persuasive writing, and presentations.

Each lesson within a unit follows a predictable structure:

- The CCSS that are covered within the lesson are listed by number.
- Materials, including all student activity pages that are needed, are also listed. It is assumed students will have access to commonplace items such as pencils and paper, so the materials noted are those items that teachers will need to obtain/acquire in advance.
- Most required readings (except picture books and read-alouds) are available in the Appendix B: Text Exemplars and Sample Performance Tasks of the CCSS ELA document. (See additional information about text selection below.) It is anticipated that using these materials will allow for easy access to appropriate readings. In many cases, the readings that are used may come from the grade-level band above that of the grade level specified for the book.
- The lesson plan includes an estimate for the time it might take to complete the lesson; however, this will vary by teacher and classroom.
- The objectives highlight what students will learn or be able to do as a result of completing the lesson.
- An overview of the lesson's content provides a quick guide to the activities in which the students will be participating.
- A description of prior knowledge needed as a prerequisite for understanding the activities in a lesson is given. The teacher should be sure the students already have a working understanding of this content before beginning the lesson. Because the intended use of the activities is for students who have already mastered the stated standards, the teacher may want to preassess prior to having students complete the activities.
- The instructional sequence provides a detailed description of what the teacher and students will do during the lesson.
- The extension activities listed provide follow-up learning opportunities for students that go beyond the lesson to provide both additional enrichment and extension. Activities may be completed by individuals or groups, and may be completed at school or at home.
- At the end of each unit, a culminating essay is presented to provide closure and to assess students' synthesis of unit ideas.

THE SELECTION OF TEXT EXEMPLARS

The text exemplars selected for the book meet the specific criteria for high-ability learners suggested by Baskin and Harris (1980). These criteria (Center for Gifted Education, 2011) include:

- The language used in texts for the gifted should be rich, varied, precise, complex, and exciting.
- Texts should be chosen with a consideration of their open-endedness and their capacity to inspire thoughtful engagement.
- Texts for the gifted should be complex so that they promote interpretive and evaluative behaviors by readers.
- Texts for the gifted should help them develop problem-solving skills and acquire methods of productive thinking.
- Texts should provide characters as role models.
- Text types should cover a full range of materials and genres. (p. 15)

TOOLS FOR ANALYZING TEXTS

For some of the activities in this book, it is recommended that the teacher have students complete the Literature Analysis Model (see Figure 1) as part of their first encounter with the text. Teachers may want to use this model with other lessons. When students read the text for the first time, they should annotate it or use text coding (Harvey & Goudvis, 2007) as a metacognitive strategy to aid in comprehension. Once this marking of the text has occurred, the student should use the Literature Analysis Model and engage in a discussion about it (or selected portions) before progressing to other lesson activities.

The Literature Analysis Model encourages students to consider seven aspects of a selection they are reading: key words, tone, mood, imagery, symbolism, key ideas, and the structure of writing (Center for Gifted Education, 2011; McKeague, 2009; National Governors Association Center for Best Practices & Council of Chief State School Officers, 2010). After reading a selection, this model helps students to organize their initial responses and provides them with a basis for discussing the piece in small or large groups. Whenever possible, students should be allowed to underline and make notes as they read the material. After marking the text, they can organize their notes into the model.

Suggested questions for completing and discussing the model are:

- **Key words:** What words are important for understanding the selection? Which words did the author use for emphasis?
- **Important ideas:** What is the main idea of the selection? What are other important ideas in the selection?
- **Tone:** What is the attitude or what are the feelings of the author toward the subject of the selection? What words does the author use to indicate tone?

HANDOUT
Literature Analysis Model

Chosen or assigned text: _____	
Key words	
Important ideas	
Tone	
Mood	
Imagery	
Symbolism	
Structure of writing	

Figure 1. Literature Analysis Model. *Note.* Adapted from *Exploring America in the 1950s* (p. 10) by M. Sandling & K. L. Chandler, 2014, Waco, TX: Prufrock Press. Copyright 2014 by Center for Gifted Education. Adapted with permission.

- **Mood:** What emotions do you feel when reading the selection? How do the setting, images, objects, and details contribute to the mood?
- **Imagery:** What are examples of the descriptive language that is used to create sensory impressions in the selection?
- **Symbolism:** What symbols are used to represent other things?
- **Structure of writing:** What are some important characteristics of the way this piece is written? How do the parts of this selection fit together and relate to each other? How do structural elements contribute to the meaning of the piece?

After students have completed their Literature Analysis Models individually, they should compare their answers in small groups. These small groups may compile a composite model that includes the ideas of all members. Following the small-group work, teachers have several options for using the models. For instance, they may ask each group to report to the class, they may ask groups to post their composite models, or they may develop a new Literature Analysis Model with the class based on the small-group work. It is important for teachers to hold a whole-group discussion as the final aspect of implementing this model as a teaching-learning device. Teachers are also encouraged to display the selection on a document camera or overhead projector as it is discussed and make appropriate annotations. The teacher should record ideas, underline words listed, and call attention to student responses visually. The teacher should conclude the discussion by asking open-ended follow-up questions. For more information about analyzing literature, see Center for Gifted Education (2011).

GROUPING OPTIONS

The lessons in this book can be used for whole-group, small-group, and individual instruction.

Whole-Group Instruction

Teachers can use this book in one academic year in conjunction with the primary curriculum in a gifted education or advanced ELA class. All students would complete each lesson after being introduced to particular content standards. Teachers can integrate the lessons into the primary curriculum taught to a whole group and address higher order thinking questions through the lesson activities.

Small-Group Instruction

Teachers can use this book to differentiate learning in any ELA class by creating flexible student groups and giving students who need enrichment an opportunity for deeper understanding and engagement with a concept. Students can complete activities and practice at a self-guided pace with a partner or small group and engage in peer discussion, with or without directed supervision or intervention from the teacher.

Individual Instruction

The activities and questions in each lesson are a good way to determine individual understanding of a certain language arts concept on a deeper level.

AUTHOR'S RATIONALE FOR THE TEXTS AND THEMES SELECTED

I first started teaching a project similar to what is included in Unit I: The Impact of Inventions on Our Lives a few years ago. I had an extremely dynamic class of students who loved to role-play, create, and present. Our curriculum called for us to study famous inventions, and I was looking for a way to include a project that would make it relevant for the students. After that first run of making our class museum, the project has slowly evolved and has been adapted to fit the Common Core State Standards.

I have always strived to include multicultural literature in my class, so when I came across *The Birchbark House* several years ago, I knew I had to use it some way. My kids fell in love with Omakayas and began devouring information about the Ojibwe and other tribes. When I first taught the novel, the kids guided me in a different direction than I had first intended because they were so interested in the culture that was presented. In writing Unit II: Remnants of a Past Life, I tried to think about what my kids liked the most and what they seemed most interested in doing.

Unit III: Nature Versus the Human Spirit started with ideas I used with the poem "Fog," which I have also taught in my class for several years as a springboard for writing. I feel like poetry in general is often difficult to include in fourth-grade curriculum in a meaningful way, so my goal was to come up with some ideas on how to use the poems in an interesting way, include some writing, and pair them with other texts. The theme of the unit allows the poems to be included along with the nonfiction text so they don't seem so out of place and isolated from other classroom activities.

For many years, I taught *The Watsons Go to Birmingham* by Christopher Paul Curtis, and one year I taught a child whose mother was a librarian and passed on a class set of *Bud, Not Buddy* to me after seeing the positive response I got from students about the Watsons. The thing the students loved the most about Curtis's characters was how "real" they were. They enjoyed their development and that comfortable feel his writing has. They were always able to picture how certain scenes played out. I chose *Bud, Not Buddy* for Unit IV: Overcoming Struggles because it is a CCSS exemplar text, but my students really seem to enjoy all of Curtis's works and characters.

Although these units can all be paired with the CCSS exemplar texts, they were written in such a way that they could be used with other fiction and nonfiction texts covering similar themes, topics, character development, and the like. As a teacher, I have gotten many ideas from others that I used with my own teaching tools, refined for my own students or jumpstarted an idea for something entirely different. I hope that this book not only provides teachers with lesson plans that can be used immediately, but also helps teachers come up with new ideas on how to incorporate the CCSS with your gifted learners.

UNIT I

The Impact of Inventions on Our Lives

This unit centers on the theme of improving quality of life through inventions of new ideas and improvements upon old ideas. Within the unit, students will explore inventions and advances in technology that have impacted and improved man's quality of life through informational texts. Students will consider people's wants and desires in order to determine what people look for when they call something an impact or an improvement on their quality of life. Students will demonstrate their growing understanding of this theme through various projects, research, informational writing, persuasive writing, and presentations.

LESSON 1.1
Conducting Research

Common Core State Standards

- W.4.7
- W.4.8
- RI.4.1
- RI.4.3
- RI.4.9

Materials

- Lesson 1.1 Exploring Nonfiction Text Features
- Lesson 1.1 Writing Research Questions
- Student copies of texts about inventions, such as:
  - *Toys! Amazing Stories Behind Some Great Inventions* by Don Wulffson
  - *About Time: A First Look at Time and Clocks* by Bruce Koscielniak
  - *Telescopes* by Colin A. Ronan
  - *100 Inventions That Made History* by DK Publishing
  - *An Illustrated Timeline of Inventions and Inventors* by Kremena T. Spengler

- Computer and Internet access
- Various websites about inventors, such as:
  - "The LEGO Group History" by LEGO (http://www.lego.com/en-us/aboutus/lego-group/the_lego_history)
  - "The History of Cameras" by Science Kids (http://www.sciencekids.co.nz/sciencefacts/photography/historyofcameras.html)
  - "The History of . . . Television" by Federal Communications Commission (http://transition.fcc.gov/cgb/kidszone/history_tv.html)

Estimated Time

- 90 minutes (with additional time set aside for research)

Objectives

In this lesson, students will:
- research by asking appropriate questions to focus on a general concept within a specific, self-selected topic, and
- read and comprehend informational texts.

Content

Students will acquire information about inventions to prove that they improved man's quality of life and complete a series of questions exploring nonfiction text features. Then they will develop their own research questions and research a topic.

Prior Knowledge

Students should have experience with the process of writing questions in order to research a topic. Students will need to have chosen a topic of interest after perusing the literature available in books or on websites.

INSTRUCTIONAL SEQUENCE

1. Facilitate a discussion about what it means to improve quality of life. Create an anchor chart for students on different ways quality of life can be improved, such as transportation, making tasks easier, medical advances, entertainment and leisure, etc.

2. Have students select books or articles on the Internet to read about inventions. Distribute Lesson 1.1 Exploring Nonfiction Text Features. Have students complete the handout, paying close attention to the idea that authors have specific reasons for what they do and do not include in their work.

3. Engage students in a class discussion about the many different inventions that they have been reading about and how they improved or impacted quality of life. Have students consider the time period in which some inventions were introduced when discussing whether or not they were an improvement or advancement.

4. Give students time to consider an invention to use as a research topic and how or why the invention was considered an improvement. After a few minutes, invite students to briefly discuss some of their ideas.

5. Help students begin generating a list of research questions based on the ideas that are shared that will focus their research on gathering information that proves their inventions are improvements. Have them consider what knowledge of the problem their inventions solved that they would need in order to justify their ideas. They should also consider what basic information someone would want or need to know about the invention if describing it.

6. Once students understand how to write research questions, give them time to write their own questions on their own topics. Distribute Lesson 1.1 Writing Research Questions. Model what good research questions look like for students, and consider creating a chart of "Great Questions" where you can write down strong examples generated by the students. Have them cross off any questions that don't fit with the idea of their inventions as an improvement.

Teacher's Note. Make sure that students understand that good research questions will not have simple "yes" or "no" answers. Students who find themselves stuck can start with the five Ws: who, what, when, where, and why.

7. Provide students with time to research answers to their questions, using books and online resources. Students should mark off their questions as they are answered on Lesson 1.1 Writing Research Questions, allowing both you and the students to keep track of progress. Occasionally check student work for clarity.

Extension Activities

Students may:

- create a magazine page advertisement on their invention, using their notes on how it improves quality of life; or
- write a news article informing people of their invention as though it was brand new, including a mock interview with the inventor about how and why he or she developed the product or idea.

LESSON 1.1
Exploring Nonfiction Text Features

Directions: Look through your book for each of the features listed in the chart. Mark "yes" or "no" to show whether you saw each item. Write a sentence or two to explain what you could tell about the book from each feature. Some hints and questions are included in the boxes to help you. Include information about why you think the author made the choice to include this text feature.

It is OK if your book does not have all of the features listed. It may still be a high-quality book even if it does not have all of these features.

Book Title: _____   **Author:** _____

Main Topic: _____

Features		Yes	No
Table of Contents and/or Chapter Titles *Hint: Look in the front of the book.*	What are some of the main topics of the book, based on the table of contents or chapter titles?		
Index and/or Glossary *Hint: Look in the back of the book.*	What are some of the important words or topics this book will tell you about?		
Headings *Hint: Look for a few words that introduce different sections or parts of the book/chapter.*	What can you tell about how the book/chapter is organized based on the headings?		
Bold or Italic Text	What kinds of words or information does the author highlight by using bold or italic text?		

The Impact of Inventions on Our Lives

Features		Yes	No
Drawings, Photographs, or Maps *Including captions.*	What kinds of pictures are included? What can you tell about the topics of the book/chapter from the pictures?		
Graphs, Charts, or Tables *Including captions.*	What kind of information is presented in graphs, charts, and tables in the book/chapter?		
Other features you noticed: _____ _____			

Based on the features noted above, what predictions can you make about the book/chapter you are about to read?

Note. Adapted from *Exploring Nonfiction: Questions and Organizers to Guide Teaching and Understanding Nonfiction Texts* (p. 5) by Center for Gifted Education, 2004, Williamsburg, VA: Author. Copyright 2004 by Center for Gifted Education. Adapted with permission.

LESSON 1.1
Writing Research Questions

Directions: Write the name of your invention in the space provided. Then, write as many interesting research questions as you can. Remember that good research questions do not have simple "yes" or "no" answers. Questions should address the five Ws: who, what, when, where, and why.

Class Topic: Inventions   **Main Idea:** How inventions have improved quality of life

My Invention: _____

My Questions to Research:

1.
2.
3.
4.

5.

6.

7.

8.

9.

10.

11.

12.

13.

14.

15.

LESSON 1.2
Exhibit Proposal

Common Core State Standards

- RI.4.1
- RI.4.9
- W.4.1.b
- W.4.4
- W.4.9

Materials

- Lesson 1.2 Exhibit Proposal
- Lesson 1.2 Exhibit Proposal Peer Checklist
- Student research from Lesson 1.1

Estimated Time

- 45 minutes

Objectives

In this lesson, students will:
- draw inferences from informational text, and
- use details from informational texts in order to justify and support an opinion.

Content

Students will showcase inventions that they researched in a museum exhibit scenario. In order for the museum to accept their inventions for display, they must write a proposal that justifies the inclusion of their invention into the museum.

Prior Knowledge

Students will need to have researched their topics in depth and have an understanding of their invention's impact and how it has improved quality of life.

INSTRUCTIONAL SEQUENCE

1. Introduce the following scenario to the class:

   > The Smithsonian Institute is preparing for an upcoming exhibit series on inventions. They are seeking proposals from experts on inventions that have impacted history for use in the series. As you have just completed extensive research on an invention, that makes you an expert! Each of you will submit a proposal to the Smithsonian that will prove why your invention deserves its own exhibit in the new series.

2. Distribute Lesson 1.2 Exhibit Proposal. Briefly discuss with students the types of information the museum might need to know to justify their invention's inclusion. Note that students are allowed to add to or modify the proposal sheet in order to showcase their inventions as best they can; the sheet is meant as a basic guide. Each invention will be different and may require varied information in order for students to completely justify its worth. This is an area in which students (and you) must decide how to proceed.

3. Have students complete Lesson 1.2 Exhibit Proposal, modifying where necessary. Students should refer back to their research from Lesson 1.1 to support the points they are trying to prove.

4. Distribute Lesson 1.2 Exhibit Proposal Peer Checklist. Ask students to share their proposals with a peer before submitting them to you. Partners should look at each other's proposal with a critical eye and give constructive feedback on whether or not they are convinced that the proposals prove an invention worthy to be placed into a museum exhibit about improving quality of life.

5. Afterward, have students discuss their answers on the peer checklist. Ask students to make any changes to their proposal they feel are necessary before submitting to the museum board.

Extension Activities

Students may:

- complete an oral presentation on their exhibit proposal, using Prezi (https://prezi.com) or PowerPoint, and invite constructive feedback from peers through oral discussion; or
- create an advertisement, using Canva (https://www.canva.com) or other means, for the Smithsonian's new exhibit series, that highlights the proposals that were accepted and advertise the series and its theme to the public.

LESSON 1.2
Exhibit Proposal

Directions: The Smithsonian Institute is seeking proposals on inventions for an upcoming exhibit series that showcases how inventions have impacted peoples' lives. Using the facts you acquired about your invention, answer the following questions in complete sentences. Write clearly and use enough detail to convince the reader that your proposal deserves a spot in the series.

Invention:	
Purpose of Proposal *What are you trying to accomplish?*	
Brief Description/ Background Information *Who invented it and when, why, and how?*	
Justification *How does it fit the purpose of the exhibit series?*	

Exhibit Plan *What will the design include? What objects will be present?*	
Exhibit Diagram *What will your exhibit look like? Draw a diagram.*	
Final Statement *Why should your proposal be considered?*	

LESSON 1.2
Exhibit Proposal Peer Checklist

Directions: Complete this form about your partner's exhibit proposal. Answer the questions with a "yes" or "no." Then, provide suggestions or comments for "no" answers if needed.

Peer's Name: _____

Peer's Invention: _____

1. Do you understand the purpose?   Yes   No

2. Does the proposal . . .
   a. tell who the inventor was?   Yes   No

   b. tell when the invention was made?   Yes   No

   c. tell why or how the invention was made?   Yes   No

3. Does the proposal explain why this invention belongs in the museum?   Yes   No

4. Does the proposal include plans that are easy to follow?   Yes   No

5. Does this proposal convince you that this invention belongs in a museum exhibit about inventions that have improved quality of life?   Yes   No

6. If you answered "no," to any question, provide suggestions or comments below.

The Impact of Inventions on Our Lives

LESSON 1.3
Creating the Exhibit

Common Core State Standards

- RI.4.1
- RI.4.3
- RI.4.9

Materials

- Lesson 1.2 Exhibit Proposal
- Lesson 1.3 Rubric: Museum Exhibit
- Student research from Lesson 1.1
- Shoeboxes
- Assortment of standard classroom supplies such as paper (of all types), coloring materials, scissors/glue, etc.
- Pictures of museum exhibits for student review
- Printer access (optional)

Estimated Time

- 120 minutes

Objectives

In this lesson, students will:
- apply knowledge about a topic to a real-world experience, and
- use information gathered from research to create a new product that is meaningful and relevant.

Content

Students will apply what they have learned to a real-world experience that shows the relevance of their research. Each student will create a museum exhibit on an improvement to man's quality of life. The exhibit should draw from the information researched in Lesson 1.1 and the ideas generated in Lesson 1.2, proving the invention was an improvement on quality of life for humans and supports the theme of the mock exhibit series. Students must think creatively and critically about how they will develop the exhibit to reflect their research and the ideas submitted in their proposal, and the final product should show a clear indication that the invention was an improvement.

Prior Knowledge

Students should have completed the research on their selected invention topics and completed Lesson 1.2 Exhibit Proposal to focus their ideas for this activity.

INSTRUCTIONAL SEQUENCE

1. Ask students to bring in a shoebox or other similarly sized box that can fit on their desk. Students should acquire a box that is no larger than their desks. Larger shoeboxes, package delivery boxes, or other similar cardboard boxes work well.
2. Return students' Lesson 1.2 Exhibit Proposals (with feedback) and distribute Lesson 1.3 Rubric: Museum Exhibit. Discuss the rubric criteria.

> ***Teacher's Note.*** An Exceeds Expectation column has been added to the rubric to encourage students to push themselves beyond standard expectations. Very few students may rank in this column.

3. Discuss what museum exhibits include and look like. Students can view pictures of museums online or, if reasonable, the class can visit a museum as a field trip. One strong online resource that students can view is the Baltimore Museum of Industry (http://thebmi.org), but there are many others resources available.
4. Allow time for students to make a rough sketch of their ideas for their exhibit. Then have them discuss their ideas with the class. Ideas should be generated from Lesson 1.2 Exhibit Proposal.
5. Students will then use classroom materials, or materials they bring from home, to create their exhibit inside their box. Remind students that although some basic information will be necessary, they are creating a museum exhibit that illustrates how their invention improved quality of life, and they must use the information they previously researched. Students may print pictures for the exhibit at your discretion.
6. Use a buddy system (groups of 2–3) to have students monitor each other. Ask them to provide feedback and constructive criticism of each other's exhibits as they create them. They are to help each other keep the topic of the exhibit in focus and ensure they are using relevant facts from their research.

Extension Activities

Students may:

- create a pamphlet to go along with their exhibit, highlighting their topic, summarizing the most interesting facts about it (it should include several pictures); or
- imagine that they are able to include a presentation or video that plays in their exhibit, which people could view as they walked through, and develop a slideshow or 2–3 minute video that highlights their invention.

NAME:_____   DATE:_____

LESSON 1.3 RUBRIC
Museum Exhibit

	Exceeds Expectations 5 points	Proficient 4 points	Developed 3 points	Emerging 2 points	Novice 1 point
Planning	Exemplifies the purpose, description, and justification provided in student proposal; improvements based on feedback and relevant, creative additions were made to original plans.	Exemplifies the purpose, description, and justification provided in student proposal; necessary improvements based on feedback were made.	Exemplifies the purpose, description, and justification provided in student proposal; some necessary improvements are required.	Not strongly connected to the original purpose, description, and justification; necessary improvements are required.	Not connected to the purpose, description, and justification provided in student proposal; several necessary improvements are required.
Organization	Shows careful consideration; information is presented appropriately and clearly; key ideas and important details from the topic are clearly seen with no additional need for oral explanation.	Shows careful consideration; information is presented appropriately and clearly; much can be learned from simply viewing the exhibit.	Shows consideration; information is presented appropriately, with only one or two modifications suggested to aid in understanding the topic from the exhibit alone.	Shows some consideration; some information is presented that can aid in understanding, with three or four modifications suggested to clarify information or better organize facts.	Shows little to no consideration with regards to its organization; information is not clear to the viewer, and several modifications are necessary to better organize and clarify the information in the exhibit.
Balance	Includes more than six unique visuals and more than six unique pieces of written information.	Includes five or six visuals and five or six pieces of written information.	Includes three or four visuals and three or four pieces of written information.	Includes two or three visuals and two or three pieces of written information, or exhibit includes three or more of one and two or fewer of the other.	Includes only one or two visuals or written information, or exhibit includes one but not the other.
Research	All parts are research based; exhibit includes appropriate labels and citations.	All parts are research based and can be supported with student research notes.	Most parts are researched based and can be supported with student research notes.	Some parts are research based and can be supported with student research notes.	Minimal evidence of research-based information; exhibit does not reflect learning from student research notes.

The Impact of Inventions on Our Lives

	Exceeds Expectations 5 points	Proficient 4 points	Developed 3 points	Emerging 2 points	Novice 1 point
Description	Includes details from multiple sources and includes facts that go beyond the original scope of the research.	Includes exemplary description of invention; no questions or additional information needed.	Includes adequate description of the invention; one or two areas of clarification or additional information were noted.	Includes a somewhat vague description of the invention; more details were necessary.	Provides little or no information on the invention.
Theme	Reflects a sharp focus on the invention as an improvement; theme is apparent through all visual aspects of exhibit.	Reflects an excellent focus on the invention as an improvement; no questions or additional information needed.	Reflects an adequate description of the invention as an improvement; one or two areas of clarification or additional information were noted.	Reflects a general or somewhat vague description of the invention as an improvement; more details were necessary to achieve an overall focus.	Reflects little or no information on the invention as an improvement.
Appearance	Laid out and organized as a real exhibit would appear; includes frames, plaques, cases, stanchions, and other student-chosen elements; great care was taken to provide an excellent overall appearance.	Laid out and organized as a real exhibit would appear, with details such as frames, plaques, cases, stanchions, etc.; no improvements noted.	Laid out and organized as a real exhibit would appear, with details such as frames, plaques, cases, stanchions, etc.; one or two improvements noted.	Somewhat laid out and organized as a real exhibit would appear; one or two extra details to give it a realistic feel; three or four areas of improvement noted.	Not laid out or organized as a real exhibit would appear; minimal extra details provided; several areas of improvement noted.
Neatness	Is neat, detailed, and polished; exhibit has no flaws and could be considered the "Showcase Piece" of the series.	Is neat, detailed, and polished; student displayed his or her very best effort.	Is mostly neat, detailed, and polished; student displayed a good effort.	Is somewhat neat and detailed; student could have made improvements to present a neater, more polished final product.	Is not neat, detailed, or polished; appears to have been put together in a rush, or student put forth minimal efforts with regard to appearance.
					_____ / 32

LESSON 1.4

Exhibit Presentation

Common Core State Standards

- RI.4.3
- RI.4.9
- SL.4.3
- SL.4.4

Materials

- Lesson 1.4 Peer Evaluation
- Lesson 1.4 Rubric: Exhibit Presentation
- Completed exhibits

Estimated Time

- 120 minutes

Objectives

In this lesson, students will:
- use facts from informational texts in order to speak knowledgeably about a topic, and
- support inferences made on the topic.

Content

Students will prepare a presentation, assuming the role of a museum tour guide in order to justify the choices made in creating their exhibits to a group of students. They will then complete a peer evaluation sheet on a selected exhibit and come together to discuss the results.

Prior Knowledge

Students will need to have completed the research, proposal, and museum exhibit. Students should have made inferences from the research on why their inventions improve man's quality of life and can use their research to justify those inferences.

INSTRUCTIONAL SEQUENCE

1. Distribute Lesson 1.4 Peer Evaluation and Lesson 1.4 Rubric: Exhibit Presentation. Discuss the criteria on each so that students are aware of the expectations.
2. Allow students time to prepare a presentation in which they assume the role of a tour guide in order to share their final project with others.

3. Assign each student a partner who will complete Lesson 1.4 Peer Evaluation for the student as he or she is presenting. Students should complete one evaluation form for the exhibit they have been assigned.

4. Designate time for students to visit each exhibit and have the "tour guide" take them through all of the important parts of the exhibit. Partners should complete Lesson 1.4 Peer Evaluation when viewing their assigned exhibit.

5. Once all of the presentations have been delivered, partners should meet and discuss Lesson 1.4 Peer Evaluation with one another.

Extension Activities

Students may:

- self-assess their presentation, using the rubric to score themselves.

Teacher's Note. Consider filming students' presentations so that they can view them later as a part of this extension activity.

LESSON 1.4
Peer Evaluation

Directions: Complete this form as your partner is presenting his or her project. Answer each question completely and honestly and explain each answer you give. For Questions 2–4, rate your partner 3 (awesome!), 2 (good job!), or 1 (needs improvement).

Peer's Name: _____

Peer's Topic: _____

1. What is your partner's topic? Give a couple of basic facts about the topic.

2. Did your partner seem knowledgeable about his or her topic?   3   2   1

3. Did your partner prove to you that the exhibit belonged in a museum about improvements to the quality of man's life?   3   2   1

4. Did your partner use his or her research to explain the invention to you?   3   2   1

5. What did you enjoy the most about this exhibit?

6. If this were your project, what would you have done differently?

The Impact of Inventions on Our Lives

LESSON 1.4 RUBRIC
Exhibit Presentation

	Exceeds Expectations 5 points	Proficient 4 points	Developed 3 points	Emerging 2 points	Novice 1 point
Speaking	Presenter was clear, used appropriate tone and inflection, and preparation was evident.	Members of the class were able to hear the presentation.	Presenter was asked to speak more loudly one or two times.	Presenter was asked to speak more loudly three or four times.	Presenter was asked to speak more loudly five or more times.
Pace	Pacing was appropriate for each element presented; changes in pacing were done appropriately and with intent; preparation was evident.	Appropriately paced throughout its entirety.	One or two parts needed a change of pace (e.g., speed up or slow down).	Three or four parts needed a change of pace.	Too fast or too slow for the task.
Confidence	Confident and maintained appropriate eye contact; appeared relaxed with mannerisms fitting an expert presenting in his or her field.	Confident and maintained appropriate eye contact.	Confident and made eye contact throughout most of the presentation.	Showed some confidence and attempted to make eye contact a few times.	Showed little or no confidence, and made minimal or no attempts at eye contact.
Theme	Sharp focus on the invention as an improvement; appropriately tied information into the theme several times.	Excellent focus on the invention as an improvement; no questions or additional information needed.	Adequate description of the invention as an improvement was provided; one or two areas of clarification or additional information were noted.	A general or somewhat vague description of the invention as an improvement was provided; more details were necessary to achieve an overall focus.	Little or no information was provided on the invention as an improvement.
Description	A well-planned and thought-out description of invention was provided with additional supporting details that exceed expectations.	A planned and thought-out basic description of invention was provided; no questions or additional information were needed.	An adequate description of the invention was provided; one or two areas of clarification or additional information were noted.	A general or somewhat vague description of the invention was provided; more details were necessary.	Little or no information was provided on the invention; student seemed unprepared.

The Impact of Inventions on Our Lives

	Exceeds Expectations 5 points	Proficient 4 points	Developed 3 points	Emerging 2 points	Novice 1 point
Research	Referenced the researched evidence more than five times during presentation; evidence clearly supported student ideas.	Referenced the researched evidence three to five times during the presentation; evidence supported student ideas.	Referenced the researched evidence twice during the presentation; evidence supported student ideas.	Referenced the researched evidence once during the presentation; evidence supported student ideas; or student referenced evidence, but evidence was not always linked to student ideas being expressed.	Did not mention evidence; or evidence did not support student ideas.
Performance	Role of tour guide exceeded expectations, in addition to the components of posture, tone of voice, structure, and movement; included other self-selected details including dress and development of character.	Completely fulfilled role of tour guide with reference to the four performance components: posture, tone of voice, structure, and movement.	Mostly fulfilled role of tour guide with reference to three of the four performance components: posture, tone of voice, structure, and movement.	Somewhat fulfilled role of tour guide with reference to two of the four performance components: posture, tone of voice, structure, and movement.	Did not fulfill role of tour guide with little reference to the four performance components: posture, tone of voice, structure, and movement.
Knowledge	Appeared comfortable during presentation and was able to answer all relevant questions completely; answers to questions showed depth of knowledge and exceeded expectations.	Appeared comfortable during presentation and was able to answer all relevant questions completely; evidence of preparation.	Appeared comfortable during the majority of the presentation and was able to answer most relevant questions; answers to questions showed evidence of preparation.	Appeared somewhat comfortable during presentation and was able to answer some relevant questions; answers to questions showed some evidence of preparation.	Did not seem well rehearsed and was unable to answer relevant questions; answers to questions showed little evidence of preparation.
					_____ / 32

The Impact of Inventions on Our Lives

LESSON 1.5

Exploring the Impact of Inventions

Common Core State Standards

- RI.4.1
- RI.4.3
- RI.4.9
- W.4.1
- W.4.4
- W.4.7
- W.4.8
- W.4.9

Materials

- Lesson 1.5 Planning Page
- Lesson 1.5 Rubric: Opinion Writing
- Student copies of texts about inventions, such as:
  - *Toys! Amazing Stories Behind Some Great Inventions* by Don Wulffson
  - *About Time: A First Look at Time and Clocks* by Bruce Koscielniak
  - *Telescopes* by Colin A. Ronan

Estimated Time

- 180 minutes

Objectives

In this lesson, students will:
- use information from multiple sources in order to form and write about an opinion, and
- use details from the text to support their ideas.

Content

Students will work in pairs to review two different inventions described in the anchor text(s). They will locate important facts about each and write a persuasive essay to form an opinion on which invention better improved the quality of life, using information from the text(s) to support their opinion statement.

Prior Knowledge

Students will need to have read the anchor texts. They should be familiar with the writing process and have had experience with persuasive writing and using information from multiple text resources.

INSTRUCTIONAL SEQUENCE

1. Ask students to select an invention of interest from the presentations that they viewed in Lesson 1.4. Then pair them with someone in the class who has a different invention. Consider having students write their choice on a piece of scrap paper to be pulled out of a hat, or use a similar random-choice strategy.

Teacher's Note. Ensure that each pair of students has access to the texts needed. Rotating centers may be required.

2. Explain to students that they will locate facts about their and their partner's invention with an emphasis on how the inventions were considered improvements. Model the note-taking strategy you want them to use to gather their facts.

3. Afterward, ask them to choose the invention they feel had the greatest impact on people's quality of life. Pairs do not need to come to a consensus; each student can make his or her own decision.

4. Facilitate a discussion about what constitutes an improvement on a person's life. As students are forming their opinions, help them focus their decisions on what is important to them, as well as what may be important to others. Guiding questions may include:
   - What is it that you are looking for when determining if something has improved your life?
   - Which invention better reflects your wants and desires?

5. Tell students that they will be writing a persuasive essay. Have students complete Lesson 1.5 Planning Page as a prewriting activity. As students are completing the chart, they may need guidance on how to complete the third column, Justification. Have them consider the following questions:
   - Does the other invention lack a particular quality that your choice does, or do you feel a particular quality is not as good or as defined?
   - Why are the wants and/or needs addressed by the other invention not as important to you?
   - Does the other invention fulfill a want whereas yours fulfills a need?

6. Distribute Lesson 1.5 Rubric: Opinion Writing. Guide students through the writing process, reminding them to articulate their opinion and support it with information they gathered from the texts. They should also explain why they feel the invention they chose had a greater impact on quality of life than the other.

7. Allow partners to check each other's work and offer feedback based on the criteria listed on Lesson 1.5 Rubric: Opinion Writing, as they are each knowledgeable about both topics they were tasked with studying.

Extension Activities

Students may:

- create an infographic on Canva (https://www.canva.com) that outlines the main ideas and supporting details from their essay that would serve as a visual element to enhance the writing; or

- analyze the importance of the inventions from the view of different subgroups—children, adults, or the elderly—and create an organizer or chart where they explain how their project choices would have changed if they focused on another age group.

LESSON 1.5
Planning Page

Directions: List the two inventions you were to choose between. Then, list the invention you chose that had a greater impact on quality of life. In the chart, list three reasons why you feel your chosen invention had the greater impact. Then, list the evidence that supports each reason. Last, justify your opinion by explaining why the other invention does not satisfy the reasons and supporting evidence listed.

Invention 1: _____

Invention 2: _____

Which invention are you choosing? _____

Reasons for My Choice	Supporting Evidence	Justification
1.	1.	1.

Challenging Common Core Language Arts Lessons: Grade 4 © Prufrock Press Inc.

Reasons for My Choice	Supporting Evidence	Justification
2.	2.	2.
3.	3.	3.

The Impact of Inventions on Our Lives

LESSON 1.5 RUBRIC
Opinion Writing

	Exceeds Expectations 9 points	Proficient 7 points	Developed 5 points	Emerging 3 points	Novice 1 point
Content	Sharply focused on the main idea that an invention has improved lives and how it reflects their wants and desires; ample details provided.	Sufficiently develops main idea and how it reflects their wants and desires; sufficient details provided.	Mostly develops main idea and how it reflects their wants and desires; some details provided.	Only somewhat develops main idea and how it reflects their wants and desires; few details provided.	Does not develop main idea that an invention has improved lives, and how it reflects their wants and desires.
Connection of Ideas	Ideas are connected with excellent clarity and critical thinking is evident; explain why one invention had a greater impact.	Ideas are sufficiently connected with good flow and clarity; explain why one invention had a greater impact.	Ideas are sometimes connected with minimal interruption to flow, attempt to explain why one invention had a greater impact.	Ideas are not well connected, paper does not flow well; minimal attempt to explain why one invention had a greater impact.	Ideas are not connected, paper is difficult to read and often does not make sense; no explanation as to why one invention had a greater impact than another.
Evidence	Use of ample, well-chosen evidence from texts to support main ideas.	Use of sufficient, well-chosen evidence from text to support main ideas	Use of evidence to support some main ideas.	Use of evidence does not support main ideas; or reads as a summary of the text.	Little or no evidence used to support main ideas.
Style	Exemplary command of opinion style, including use of persuasive language and interesting and varying sentence patterns.	Sufficient command of opinion style, including use of persuasive language and varying sentence patterns.	Adequate command of opinion style, including some use of persuasive language.	Weak command of opinion style; little use of persuasive language; language is sometimes unclear.	Little or no command of opinion style; very limited or no persuasive language.
Conventions of Writing	No mistakes in grammar, mechanics, or spelling.	One mistake in grammar and/or spelling.	Two or three mistakes in grammar and/or spelling.	Four or five mistakes in grammar and/or spelling.	More than five mistakes in grammar and/or spelling.
					_____ / 35

LESSON 1.6
Redesigning Inventions for Further Improvement

Common Core State Standards

- RI.4.1
- SL.4.1
- SL.4.3
- SL.4.4

Materials

- Lesson 1.6 Redesign
- Lesson 1.6 Rubric: Redesign Product
- Student copies of texts about inventions, such as
  - *Toys! Amazing Stories Behind Some Great Inventions* by Don Wulffson
  - *About Time: A First Look at Time and Clocks* by Bruce Koscielniak
  - *Telescopes* by Colin A. Ronan

- Computer and Internet access

Estimated Time

- 45 minutes

Objectives

In this lesson, students will:
- choose appropriate facts from the text to support and explain an opinion.

Content

Students will select inventions that they feel can be improved upon to better fit today's society. They will discuss with one another what people need, want, and desire in today's world, and choose an invention that they feel has the most potential for improvement based on the facts presented. They will then explain what they would want to improve and how and justify their choices by explaining how their improvement would make it better match those needs, wants, and desires they discussed.

Prior Knowledge

Students should have experience selecting appropriate information from texts. Students also should have preestablished protocols for group discussions.

INSTRUCTIONAL SEQUENCE

1. Ask students to refer to the texts and make a list of inventions that they feel could be further improved upon to better accommodate the current needs of society. (This may or may not be the inventions they used in previous activities.) Students should consider only inventions that could be improved upon in a realistic manner.

2. Allow students to further research their inventions on the Internet and find out if any improvements have already been made, or gain more facts that would help them decide how to improve them.

3. Independently, in pairs, or in small groups, have students select an invention they feel has the most potential for improvement.

4. Facilitate a whole-class or group discussion about what kinds of improvements to current objects, tools, machines, or technology might benefit people in today's world. Have them consider the games they like to play, the technology they like to use, things they like to do outside of school, and so forth.

5. As students discuss modifications and improvements, they can use Lesson 1.6: Redesign to keep their ideas aligned with what they learned through their research. The "How I Would Justify My Decision" section should show a clear connection to their discussions on improvements that would benefit people in today's world. The explanation should explain not only why they chose to make the improvement, but also why it is a better match for the needs of today's society.

6. Once students have completed Lesson 1.6: Redesign, have them share their ideas with the rest of the class. Idea sharing can take many forms, including a formal presentation, a commercial to advertise the new and improved invention, poster board, video, and the like. Distribute and review Lesson 1.6 Rubric: Redesign Product before students begin.

Extension Activities

Students may:

- complete another product, such as a poster, 3-D model, or an infomercial and deliver an oral presentation that may include a Prezi or Powerpoint; or

- read *Tuck Everlasting* by Natalie Babbitt, exploring the idea of a fountain of youth as an invention and its superficial effects on people versus the more practical uses of other inventions in this unit. Have students make a list of the uses and benefits of the fountain of youth and label each as superficial or practical. Then they should look at the fountain's impact of the characters in *Tuck Everlasting* by creating character maps and create a chart or write an essay on the positive and negative effects that could be seen if such an idea were introduced to people today.

LESSON 1.6
Redesign

Directions: After choosing an invention and discussing the wants and needs of today's society, construct a list of at least three things you would improve about your invention. Complete each part of this worksheet, explaining what you think should be improved, how you would improve it, and why.

Invention: _____

Facts About My Invention

How I Would Improve It

The Impact of Inventions on Our Lives

How I Would Justify My Decision

LESSON 1.6 RUBRIC
Redesign Product

	Exceeds Expectations 5 points	Proficient 4 points	Developed 3 points	Emerging 2 points	Novice 1 point
Facts	Demonstrates more than three facts on the invention that align with the redesign plan; additional facts enhance the description beyond expectations.	Demonstrates an excellent description of three basic facts of the invention that align with the redesign plan.	Demonstrates an adequate description of three basic facts of the invention that mostly align with the redesign plan.	Demonstrates a general description of three basic facts of the invention that somewhat align with the redesign plan.	Demonstrates little or no description of three basic facts of the invention; facts are vague and/or do not align with the redesign plan.
Invention Improvements	Demonstrates more than three articulate and thoughtful invention improvements that completely align with the facts.	Demonstrates three well-planned and thoughtful invention improvements that align with the selected facts.	Demonstrates three thoughtful invention improvements that align with the selected facts; ideas may require more focus and planning.	Demonstrates three invention improvements that somewhat align with the selected facts, improvements may be lacking in focus and require additional information.	Demonstrates little or no thought to invention improvements; ideas are vague, unrealistic, or lacking in thought and purpose.
Justification of Ideas	Demonstrates a sharp and well-thought out justification for more than three improvements that are realistic, thoughtful, and sharply aligned with the facts presented.	Demonstrates an excellent justification for three improvements that are realistic, thoughtful, and align with the facts presented on the invention.	Demonstrates an adequate justification for three improvements that are mostly realistic, and mostly align with the facts presented on the invention.	Demonstrates a general justification for three improvements that somewhat align with the facts presented on the invention; ideas may not be realistic.	Demonstrates little or no justification for three improvements, ideas are vague, not realistic, and/or do not align with the facts presented on the invention.
					_____ / 12

The Impact of Inventions on Our Lives

UNIT I
Culminating Essay Prompt

Directions: In this unit, you have researched inventions and how they improved quality of life. It is 15 years in the future. You are now an adult. Considering the inventions you studied, how would each fit into some aspect of your daily life? Write a narrative about a day or week in your life during which you use each invention you studied. Your narrative should show the benefits of each invention to your life, and include realistic modifications to the inventions that occurred over the last 15 years.

The Impact of Inventions on Our Lives

UNIT II

Remnants of a Past Life

This unit centers on themes related to the unintended effects of westward expansion on Native American tribes and their cultures. Within the unit, students will read, analyze, evaluate, and interpret a novel and nonfiction texts with themes related to how Native American cultures have changed or stayed the same since westward expansion. They will consider aspects of cultures that are still present today and aspects that have become memories of a past life, as they work to develop an appreciation for historical fiction and recognizing events from fiction that accurately reflect real events of a time period. Students will demonstrate their growing understanding of this theme through various projects, narrative writing, informational writing, and persuasive writing.

LESSON 2.1
What Happened After Smallpox?

Common Core State Standards

- W.4.3
- RL.4.1
- RI.4.1
- RI.4.8

Materials

- Lesson 2.1 Effects of Expansion
- Lesson 2.1 Narrative Writing Content Planning (optional)
- Lesson 2.1 Rubric: Narrative Writing
- Student copies of *The Birchbark House* by Louise Erdrich
- Student copies of *A History of US: The First Americans* by Joy Hakim (optional)
- Computer and Internet access
- Online resources, such as:
    - "Ojibwe Language & Culture" (http://www.pbs.org/indiancountry/challenges/ojibwe.html)
    - "More Ojibwe History" (http://www.ojibwe.org/home/about_anish_more.html)
    - "American Expansion" (http://publications.newberry.org/indiansofthemidwest/people-places-time/eras/american-expansion)
    - "Ojibwe History" (https://www.mpm.edu/wirp/ICW-151.html)

Estimated Time

- 120 minutes (with additional time set aside for research)

Objectives

In this lesson, students will:
- write a narrative to extend a historical fiction story, using facts acquired from the text and other informational sources.

Content

Students will write a narrative passage, extending a text, *The Birchbark House*, beyond the end of the story. They will use research to predict what may have happened to the main character, Omakayas's, tribe after smallpox—what changed and what stayed the same (or even what they may have tried to preserve).

Prior Knowledge

Students will need to have read *The Birchbark House* by Louise Erdrich and have practice with locating information in text and online. Students should have prior exposure to narrative writing style and the writing process.

INSTRUCTIONAL SEQUENCE

1. Ensure that students understand that smallpox was a real disease that affected many Native American tribes like Omakayas's in *The Birchbark House*. Discuss difficulties caused by settlers that affected Native American tribes, including disease, fighting, encroachment, and relocation.

2. Have students research the Ojibwe and/or Anishinaabe, as presented in *The Birchbark House*, using online resources, the section on "Plains Indians are Not Indians at All" in *A History of US: The First Americans*, and/or any other books you may have on the topic. Focus the research on factors that were directly related to the U.S. westward expansion. Students should note what those factors were, how they affected the tribe, and what the results were.

3. Distribute Lesson 2.1 Effects on Expansion. Guide students to consider things like loss of animals for hunting due to European settlement, attempts to assimilate Native Americans into European culture, especially in education and religion, negotiations for land and reservations, Native Americans that began to work for wages, and customs that were declared illegal by the United States government.

Teacher's Note. You may choose for students to complete the entire chart, or ask them to complete a minimum of five sections on the chart, depending on what information they are able to locate. There is a wealth of information on this topic and students may conduct research using exemplar texts, online resources, or library books. Students may work in small groups, in pairs, or independently.

4. Have students work in groups to discuss their findings and make inferences. Drawing upon evidence from *The Birchbark House* and their research, students should determine what traditions might have been affected by westward expansion.

5. Then have students choose one effect of westward expansion on the tribe and complete a narrative writing task, responding to the following prompt:

> After smallpox, Omakayas's family and tribe are left to pick up the pieces. However, this is not the end of their troubles; settlers continue to expand west and bring with them new threats. Consider what was left of their tribe after smallpox, and how customs, traditions, or ways of life were affected. How does this new threat present itself, and how does it further complicate the tribe's ability to deal with the aftermath of smallpox and move on?

> **Teacher's Note.** In order to complete this writing task, attention to proper prewriting activities and ideas is essential. Students should utilize discussion and sharing of work to help them focus on the many components presented in the task. Lesson 2.1 Narrative Writing Content Planning can be used to help students get started.

6. Students should utilize *The Birchbark House* not only to identify the customs and traditions, but also to continue the story with a similar style and the same attention to the characters' traits and actions. Distribute Lesson 2.1 Rubric: Narrative Writing before students begin.

Extension Activities

Students may:
- read the next book in the series, *The Game of Silence* by Louise Erdrich, and compare it to their ideas in the narrative by creating a graphic organizer (such as a Venn diagram) and draft a constructed response explaining how close their predictions were; or
- write a mythical story or about a dream that foreshadows the new threat they wrote about in their narrative, keeping in mind that the myth or dream should not be a literal explanation of what's to come, but rather a seemingly unrelated myth or legend that draws a comparison with a similar conflict.

LESSON 2.1
Effects of Expansion

Directions: Complete the chart, using the factors listed in the first column and the information you researched on the effects of westward expansion in the second and third columns. List any additional factors you discovered in your research in the last two rows. These rows are not required, but you should complete them if you have additional information.

Factors	How Was This Problematic?	What Were the Long-Term Effects?
Smallpox		
Animals		
Assimilation		
Land Negotiations		

Factors	How Was This Problematic?	What Were the Long-Term Effects?
Wage Labor		
Customs Declared Illegal		

NAME:_____ DATE:_____

LESSON 2.1
Narrative Writing Content Planning

Directions: After smallpox, Omakayas's family and tribe are left to pick up the pieces. However, this is not the end of their troubles; settlers continue to expand west and bring with them new threats. Consider what was left of their tribe after smallpox, and how it affected customs, traditions, or ways of life. How does this new threat present itself, and how does it further complicate the tribe's ability to deal with the aftermath of smallpox and move on?

Use this prompt and the questions below to plan your narrative.

Planning Questions

1. Based on my research, smallpox has affected the Ojibwe tribe's way of life in the following ways:

2. I have included a new threat to the tribe:

3. List the customs, traditions, and/or ways of life that will be affected:

4. This threat will affect the customs, traditions, and/or ways of life because (provide evidence from the text):

Remnants of a Past Life

NAME:_____ DATE:_____

LESSON 2.1 RUBRIC
Narrative Writing

	Exceeds Expectations 9 points	Proficient 7 points	Developed 5 points	Emerging 3 points	Novice 1 point
Content	Sharply focused on the new threat introduced to Omakayas's family, how it affected their ways of life, and how it complicated their ability to deal with the aftermath of smallpox, with exceptional use of details.	Sufficiently develops the new threat introduced to Omakayas's family and how it affected their ways of life, with sufficient use of details to express ideas.	Mostly develops the new threat introduced to Omakayas's family and attempts to develop how it affected their ways of life, with some use of details to express ideas.	Only somewhat develops the new threat introduced to Omakayas's family and somewhat attempts to develop how it affected their ways of life, with minimal details.	Does not develop the new threat introduced to Omakayas's family or how it affected their ways of life; very limited use of details.
Development of Characters	Characters are exceptionally developed with consideration of thoughts, actions, behaviors, and exceptional use of dialogue.	Characters are sufficiently developed with consideration of actions, behaviors, and sufficient use of dialogue.	Characters are somewhat developed with consideration of actions, behaviors, and some use of dialogue.	Characters are minimally developed with some consideration of actions, behaviors, and little use of dialogue.	Characters are not developed with no consideration of actions, behaviors, or use of dialogue.
Evidence	Use of ample, well-chosen evidence from texts to support main ideas.	Use of sufficient, well-chosen evidence from text to support main ideas.	Use of evidence to support some main ideas.	Use of evidence does not support main ideas, or student work reads as a summary of the text.	Little or no evidence used to support main ideas.
Style	Exemplary command of narrative style, including establishment of character, setting, and situation, with a natural flow.	Sufficient command of narrative style, including establishment of character, setting, and situation, with a natural flow.	Adequate command of narrative style which includes establishment of character, setting, and situation, with a mostly natural flow.	Weak command of narrative style, including establishment of character, setting, and situation, with little natural flow.	Little or no command of narrative style, including establishment of character, setting, and situation, with no natural flow.
Conventions of Writing	No mistakes in grammar, mechanics, or spelling.	One mistake in grammar and/or spelling.	Two or three mistakes in grammar and/or spelling.	Four or five mistakes in grammar and/or spelling.	More than five mistakes in grammar and/or spelling.
					_____ / 35

Remnants of a Past Life

LESSON 2.2
Traditions Maintained

Common Core State Standards

- RI.4.1
- RI.4.8
- RI.4.9
- RL.4.1
- RL.4.3
- L.4.3
- W.4.7
- W.4.8

Materials

- Lesson 2.2 Traditions Maintained
- Lesson 2.2 Compare and Contrast
- Student copies of *The Birchbark House* by Louise Erdrich
- Computer and Internet access
- Online resources, such as:
  - "Ojibwe Language & Culture" (http://www.pbs.org/indiancountry/challenges/ojibwe.html)
  - "Ojibwe History" (http://www.mpm.edu/wirp/ICW-51.html)
  - "More Ojibwe History" (http://www.ojibwe.org/home/about_anish_more.html)

Estimated Time

- 90 minutes

Objectives

In this lesson, students will:
- locate information in a fictional text and support/extend that information with facts gathered from nonfiction text(s) to write effectively about a topic, and
- compare and contrast the Ojibwe way of life from the 19th century to the Ojibwe today using information from multiple sources.

Content

Students will examine traditions from *The Birchbark House* that are still maintained today by the Ojibwe tribe. They will create a chart outlining traditions evidenced in *The Birchbark House* and research located in other texts. Then they will read about the Ojibwe today to determine what customs and/or traditions are still practiced. Then, they will compare and contrast the Ojibwe of

Omakayas's time to the Ojibwe tribe today and use their comparison to articulate what customs have died out and how remaining customs are still observed.

Prior Knowledge

Students will need to have read the anchor text *The Birchbark House*. Students should be familiar enough with the text to locate information in it quickly and easily. Students should understand how to cite sources of information.

INSTRUCTIONAL SEQUENCE

1. Have students work with partners to locate different customs and traditions that were presented in *The Birchbark House*. Distribute Lesson 2.2 Traditions Maintained. Have students begin by completing the first two columns on which traditions they located in the text and how they were observed.
2. Students may also add anything learned from nonfiction texts about the Ojibwe during the same time period. If students are recording information from multiple texts, ask them to list their sources on the back of the handout.
3. Referring to online resources, ask students to circle or highlight which traditions on their chart have evidence of continuation today. In the last column, they should describe how that tradition is observed today, and also list which sources they used as before.
4. Students will then use the chart to compare and contrast the Ojibwe of the early 19th century to the Ojibwe today, using Lesson 2.2 Venn Diagram.
5. Differentiate by letting students choose their own method of presenting the information.
6. Have students participate in a student-led discussion, inferring why some traditions were maintained and others died out. Guiding questions may include:
   - Do you notice any common factors between the traditions that were maintained? Were there any common factors between traditions that died out?
   - How did the Ojibwe manage to maintain certain traditions?
   - What were factors that may have caused other traditions to die out?
   - Were these factors under anyone's control?
   - Did the Ojibwe allow any traditions to fade? Why or why not?

Extension Activities

Students may:
- further research the impact on the Ojibwe, or other tribe of interest, and develop a trifold poster, covering how westward expansion affected a particular Native American tribe, comparing how that tribe used to live to how they live today.

LESSON 2.2
Traditions Maintained

Directions: In the first column, list traditions and customs you observed in your reading of *The Birchbark House*. In the middle column, describe how that tradition was observed. Once you have completed your research, you will highlight the traditions in column one that have evidence of continuation. In the last column, use your research to describe how these customs and traditions are observed today. List your sources on the back of this handout.

Traditions	How They Were Observed	Evidence of Continuation

Remnants of a Past Life

Traditions	How They Were Observed	Evidence of Continuation

NAME:_____ DATE:_____

LESSON 2.2
Compare and Contrast

Directions: Use this Venn diagram to compare and contrast the Ojibwe from the early 19th-century to the Ojibwe today.

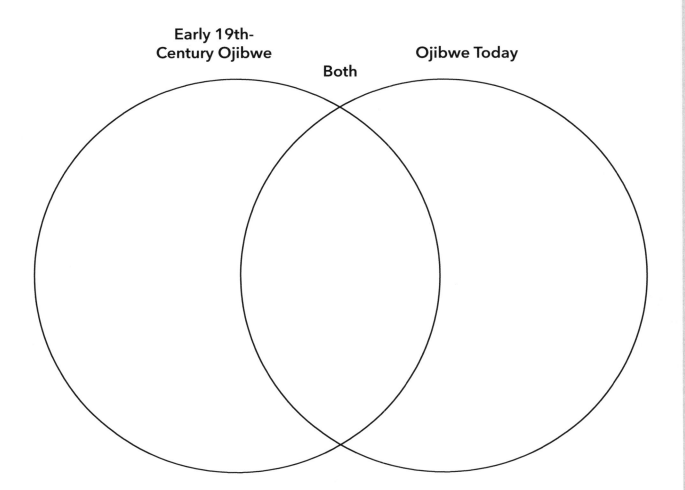

Early 19th-Century Ojibwe

Both

Ojibwe Today

Remnants of a Past Life

LESSON 2.3

"Not Just the Ojibwe": Broadening the Scope

Common Core State Standards

- RL.4.1
- RI.4.1
- RI.4.9
- W.4.7
- W.4.9
- SL.4.1

Materials

- Lesson 2.3 Venn Diagrams
- Student copies of *The Birchbark House* by Louise Erdrich
- Student copies of *A History of US: The First Americans* by Joy Hakim (optional)
- Student copies of *A History of US: The New Nation* by Joy Hakim (optional)
- Informational books on other Native American tribes chosen by students
- Computer and Internet access
- Online resources, such as "Native American Tribes" (http://www.legendsofamerica.com/na-tribes.html)
- A map of Native American tribes (http://www.tribalnationsmaps.com includes an excellent map that can be viewed online or purchased for repeated use)
- Index cards (one per student, pair, or group)

Estimated Time

- 120 minutes

Objectives

In this lesson, students will:
- research to acquire information on a topic from multiple texts in order to make inferences, and
- communicate ideas orally and in writing.

Content

Students will look at customs and traditions left from the Ojibwe tribe and compare them to other Native American tribes that were affected by westward expansion, deciding whether or not the effects were similar.

Prior Knowledge

Students will need to have read *The Birchbark House*. Students should be able to locate information in books or on websites with minimal assistance. Students should understand effective communication (speaking and listening skills) during class discussion (accountable talk).

INSTRUCTIONAL SEQUENCE

1. Display a map of Native American tribes and allow students to choose a tribe in a different region from the Ojibwe. Students can also select a tribe they read about in one of Joy Hakim's *A History of US* volumes. This can be done independently, in pairs, or in small groups. Encourage students to select a variety of different tribes.

2. Allow students to perform online research or check out books from the school library on their chosen tribe. They should locate information about the tribe's historical traditions and customs and which of those are still observed today.

3. As students are researching, have them complete the following statement on an index card: "The _____ tribe was affected by westward expansion because _____." Display these where all students can see them.

4. After students have gathered their information, distribute Lesson 2.3 Venn Diagrams. Students will compare and contrast their new tribe to what they know about the Ojibwe in the first Venn diagram. As they work, visit with students to see if they are on track and assist as necessary. Is one section particularly full or empty, and what observations/conclusions can they draw from that?

5. Increase complexity by placing two students (or pairs or groups) with different tribes together and repeat using the triple Venn diagram on Lesson 2.3 Venn Diagrams. Ask students to make similar observations and conclusions as they work.

6. Facilitate a whole-class discussion about the student observations recorded on the Venn diagrams. Examine themes and information that are similar and discuss why some traditions may be easier to maintain than others. Also have students discuss the factors that may have influenced which traditions survived and which did not.

7. Refer students back to the index cards they completed earlier in the lesson. Guiding questions may include:
   - Do you notice any similarities in what you wrote on the cards across the many different tribes?
   - Are there any differences?

This will serve as the basis for a variety of different topics for discussion when looking closely at the consequences of expansion, both intended and unintended.

8. Refer back to the previous lessons using *The Birchbark House* and Omakaya's family. Be sure students understand that the information presented in the text was not an isolated event, but part of a larger picture as the U.S. expanded west.

Extension Activities

Students may:
- create a flowchart for sequence or a cause/effect chart that explains traditions of the Ojibwe and other tribes that have been modified or adapted, the reasons for modification and

adaptation, and the benefits of the modifications and adaptations to maintaining the tribes' cultures; or

- develop a timeline of events that includes actions of European settlers that affected Native Americans and any documented responses, such as wars or fights, resettlements, government actions, etc.

LESSON 2.3
Venn Diagrams

Directions: Use the Venn diagram to compare and contrast the Ojibwe with your selected tribe. Then, take it one step further, and compare the Ojibwe to two other tribes in the triple Venn diagram on the following page.

Venn Diagram

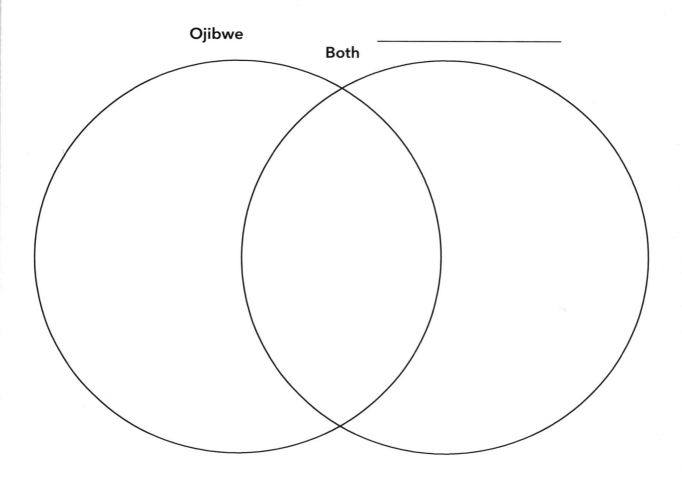

Challenging Common Core Language Arts Lessons: Grade 4 © Prufrock Press Inc.
Permission is granted to photocopy or reproduce this page for single classroom use only.

Triple Venn Diagram

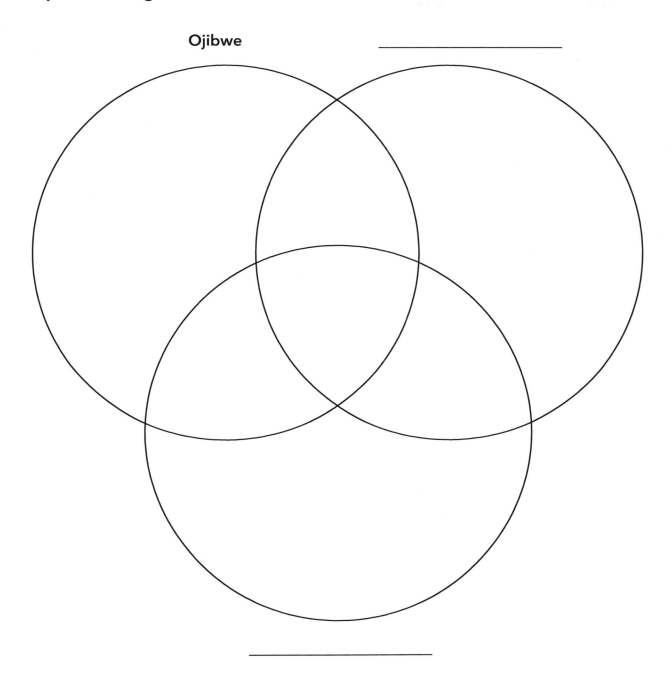

Ojibwe

_____

_____

LESSON 2.4
Put on a Play

Common Core State Standards

- SL.4.4
- SL.4.5
- RL.4.1
- RL.4.2
- RL.4.3
- RL.4.5
- RL.4.7

Materials

- Lesson 2.4 Play Planning
- Lesson 2.4 Script Writing (optional)
- Lesson 2.4 Peer Feedback
- Lesson 2.4 Rubric: Playwriting
- Student copies of *The Birchbark House* by Louise Erdrich
- Teacher's resource: "Teaching Playwriting in Schools" (http://www.centerstage.org/portals/0/pdf/06playwrightshandbook.pdf)

Estimated Time

- 120 minutes (with additional time set aside for playwriting)

Objectives

In this lesson, students will:
- use information and thematic elements in order to write a narrative that extends ideas found in a text.

Content

Students will use narrative writing skills to create a play, using information from both the fiction anchor text as well as nonfiction text that tells the effects of smallpox on families such as Omakayas's. The play will be closely tied to the theme of unintended effects of westward expansion, and students will select details and/or facts that support the theme throughout.

Prior Knowledge

Students will need to have read *The Birchbark House*. Students should be familiar with narrative writing. Students should also know the elements of a play and be able to apply that knowledge in order to write their own mini scripts.

INSTRUCTIONAL SEQUENCE

Teacher's Note. You may visit "Teaching Playwriting in Schools" (http://www.centerstage.org/portals/0/pdf/06playwrightshandbook.pdf) for ideas on how to help your students write a play. Although designed for students to submit work to a festival, it contains a wealth of information on helping students write plays.

1. Divide students into groups of 3–5. Explain that each group will create a play focusing on the theme of unintended consequences of westward expansion. Ask: *If you were to choose four scenes from* The Birchbark House *that supported this theme, which scenes would they be and why?*

2. Have students complete Lesson 2.4 Play Planning and submit for your review.

3. Then have students write a script for each scene, using a narrative drama style. Distribute Lesson 2.4 Script Writing for students who need assistance getting started. They will need one sheet for each scene. Please note to students that this page is to help them begin, and they may wish to include additional plot points and/or stage directions when they begin writing.

4. Distribute Lesson 2.4 Rubric: Playwriting before students begin writing. As students work, discuss literary elements from the novel that should be presented in each scene, including characters, details of the setting, tone or mood, dialogue taken from the text, directions on mannerisms, and so forth. This is a great place to focus on any literary elements that may benefit students; however, make sure the purpose of the writing is geared toward the theme of unintended consequences.

Teacher's Note. Characters can include any main characters of the story, like Omakayas, Pinch, DeyDey, Mama, Nokomis, Angeline, or characters important to a scene such as Neewo, Old Tallow, Fishtail, or Ten Snow. Details from the setting should include descriptions taken from the text or the images that accompany the text. Students should also recognize that for this activity, they will use sections of the text that have a sad, desperate, or hopeless tone. This should also show up in the way in which they discuss character mannerisms and behaviors. Other literary elements to discuss can include point of view, figurative language, symbolism, or foreshadowing.

5. Students in each group can provide feedback and constructive criticism to other groups before submitting the scripts to you for approval. Ask them to reflect upon their work: *Does this show an unintended consequence of expansion on the Ojibwe? Is the unintended effect of expansion easily identifiable in each scene? Is the script organized and easy to understand?*

6. Have students prepare to present their plays to the class. Consider encouraging them to develop props, costumes, or backdrops at your discretion, as these would tie in additional standards. Allow students sufficient time to prepare and practice, as determined by any other elements you allow them to add to their presentations.

7. Students should complete Lesson 2.4 Peer Feedback for each group as it performs.

Extension Activities

Students may:

- write a series of diary entries as an adult Omakayas, reflecting on the events of her childhood as she has looked back and realized the effect the Europeans had on her people; or
- rewrite each scene of their play in a different format, such as a poem or song, exploring the thoughts and feelings the characters have as events occur.

LESSON 2.4
Play Planning

Directions: Complete each section below with your plans for your play. For each scene, list the characters, setting, tone, and event you intend to portray, and then write a sentence explaining how your scene will support the theme of the unintended consequences of expansion on the Ojibwe.

Group Members: _____

1. Scene 1
   a. Characters:

   b. Setting:

   c. Tone:

   d. Event:

   e. How Scene 1 supports the theme:

2. Scene 2
   a. Characters:

   b. Setting:

   c. Tone:

   d. Event:

Remnants of a Past Life

    e. How Scene 2 supports the theme:

3. Scene 3
    a. Characters:

    b. Setting:

    c. Tone:

    d. Event:

    e. How Scene 3 supports the theme:

4. Scene 4
    a. Characters:

    b. Setting:

    c. Tone:

    d. Event:

    e. How Scene 4 supports the theme:

LESSON 2.4
Script Writing

Directions: Use this handout to begin writing your script for each scene. First, fill in the scene number and the names of the characters. Number your characters in the list so that when you fill out stage directions, you can refer back to the characters. Next, figure out how you want your scene to begin, what will occur during the middle, and how you want it to end. Include any stage directions you wish to give each character. Write the character lines on a separate sheet of paper and attach this page to the front when you are finished. Be sure to include your stage directions at the appropriate points in your scripts.

1. Scene: _____

   a. The characters (number each one):

   b. How the scene will start:

   c. What main event(s) will occur during the middle:

   d. How the scene will end:

Remnants of a Past Life

2. Stage directions: (What will each character in this scene do, and how will he or she do it?)
   a. Character 1:

   b. Character 2:

   c. Character 3:

   d. Character 4:

   e. Character 5:

   List additional characters and directions below.

LESSON 2.4
Peer Feedback

Directions: Answer each question with "yes," "no," or "sometimes." Leave a constructive comment to explain your answer.

Group Presenting: _____

1. Were you able to identify the unintended effect of expansion presented in each scene?

                              Yes   No   Sometimes

   Comments:

2. Did you find the performance to be organized and easy to understand?

                              Yes   No   Sometimes

   Comments:

Remnants of a Past Life

3. Did the performers speak clearly at an understandable pace?

                        Yes   No   Sometimes

Comments:

4. Did the performers use speech and language that was appropriate for the characters?

                        Yes   No   Sometimes

Comments:

5. Do you have any additional comments for the group?

LESSON 2.4 RUBRIC
Playwriting

	Exceeds Expectations 9 points	Proficient 7 points	Developed 5 points	Emerging 3 points	Novice 1 point
Content	Develops at least four scenes that are sharply focused on unintended consequences with exemplary development based on events from the text.	Develops four scenes that are focused on unintended consequences with sufficient development based on events from the text.	Mostly develops four scenes that show some focus on unintended consequences with some development based on events from the text.	Only somewhat develops four scenes that show minimal focus on unintended consequences with minimal development based on events from the text.	Does not develop four scenes, shows limited or no focus on unintended consequences, with limited or no development based on events from the text.
Development of Ideas	Characters, setting, tone, and events are exceptionally developed with thoughtful, creative, and well-planned stage directions.	Characters, setting, tone, and events are sufficiently developed with well-planned stage directions.	Characters, setting, tone, and events are somewhat developed with adequate stage directions.	Characters, setting, tone, and events are minimally developed with few stage directions.	Characters, setting, tone, and events are not well-developed with little or no stage directions.
Evidence	Uses ample, well-chosen evidence from text to support main ideas.	Uses sufficient, well-chosen evidence from text to support main ideas.	Uses evidence to support some main ideas.	Evidence does not support main ideas, or reads exactly as the text.	Uses little or no evidence to support main ideas.
Style	Exemplary command of narrative style that includes establishment of character, setting, and situation, with a natural flow.	Sufficient command of narrative style that includes establishment of character, setting, and situation, with a natural flow.	Adequate command of narrative style that includes establishment of character, setting, and situation, with a mostly natural flow.	Weak command of narrative style that includes establishment of character, setting, and situation, with little natural flow.	Little or no command of narrative style that includes establishment of character, setting, and situation, with no natural flow.
Conventions of Writing	No mistakes in grammar, mechanics, or spelling.	One mistake in grammar and/or spelling.	Two or three mistakes in grammar and/or spelling.	Four or five mistakes in grammar and/or spelling.	More than five mistakes in grammar and/or spelling.
					_____ / 35

UNIT II
Culminating Essay Prompt

Directions: In this unit, you have studied how *The Birchbark House* reflected the unintended effects of westward expansion on the Ojibwe, and researched information on the effects of westward expansion on multiple Native American tribes. Using all of the information you have collected in your research, write an informative essay on three tribes and how expansion affected each one, drawing comparisons between them. Your essay should also describe what life is like for each tribe today. Identify key words in your writing and underline them (or use boldface if typing) to create a glossary to accompany your final product.

Nature Versus the Human Spirit

This unit centers on nature and the different effects it can have on people—how it can cause fear or a mood change for the better. Within the unit, students will read, analyze, evaluate, and interpret poetry and nonfiction texts with themes related to natural events and disasters and how they impact the human spirit. They will consider how natural disasters can impact people who live near where they occur, their negative effects, and how people have learned to deal with the effects. Students will demonstrate their growing understanding of this theme through various projects, narrative writing, informational writing, persuasive writing, and poetry.

LESSON 3.1

Interpretations of "Dust of Snow"

Common Core State Standards

- RL.4.1
- RL.4.2
- RL.4.4
- RL.4.5

Materials

- Lesson 3.1 Literature Analysis Model
- Lesson 3.1 Rubric: Frost-Style Poem
- Student copies of "Dust of Snow" by Robert Frost
- Computer and Internet access (optional)

Estimated Time

- 30–60 minutes

Objectives

In this lesson, students will:
- demonstrate understanding of the theme and structure of a poem through developing and presenting his or her own written version of the poem.

Content

The poem is about how a simple event changes the mood of the speaker. Students will go through different scenarios in which one could be having a bad day, but something unexpected caused a sudden change of heart. Students will be challenged to write their own versions of the poem, using Frost's structure of rhyme scheme and meter.

Prior Knowledge

Students will need to have read "Dust of Snow" by Robert Frost and studied its vocabulary to understand how the speaker's bad day has suddenly gotten better.

INSTRUCTIONAL SEQUENCE

1. Begin with a whole-class reading of the poem "Dust of Snow" by Robert Frost. For an initial analysis of the poem, work with the students to complete Lesson 3.1 Literature

Analysis Model. (See pp. 3–4 for additional information about using the Literature Analysis Model.)

2. Once students have completed the Literature Analysis Model and have identified any unknown words in the poem, examine the structure for the rhyme scheme of the poem (every other line rhyming) and the meter (written in diameter, with two accented syllables per line).

3. Tell students that they will be responsible for coming up with some different ideas of how bad days can be suddenly made better by something as simple as having snow shaken down off a tree branch—days where you are put in a bad mood and just need a small reminder that all will be well. Have them share some examples of bad days and the simple things that changed their moods.

4. Have students write their own version of the poem, following the determined rhyme scheme and meter. Their stanza will be about a simple event that causes the speaker to change his or her mood. Students will need to play around with their words and ideas to fit the rhyme scheme and meter used. Suggestions include adding adjectives, adverbs, or articles; removing unnecessary words; and using synonyms with more or less syllables.

5. Share finished poems at a poetry reading, or have students publish and illustrate their poems using technology.

Extension Activities

Students may:

- continue the student-generated poems with two or three more verses, in the same rhyme scheme and meter, that show the speaker of the poem, in a much better mood, "paying it forward" to another person or animal he or she passes with a simple act of kindness; or

- explore other poems by Robert Frost and analyze them for different poetry elements and meaning; his poems are often about nature and students can compare/contrast the use of nature and/or themes.

LESSON 3.1
Literature Analysis Model

Directions: Complete this Literature Analysis Model about "Dust of Snow" by Robert Frost.

"Dust of Snow" by Robert Frost	
Key Words	
Important Ideas	
Tone	
Mood	
Imagery	
Symbolism	
Structure	

Note. Adapted from *Exploring America in the 1950s* (p. 10) by M. Sandling & K. L. Chandler, 2014, Waco, TX: Prufrock Press. Copyright 2014 by Center for Gifted Education. Adapted with permission.

Nature Versus the Human Spirit

LESSON 3.1 RUBRIC

Frost-Style Poem

	Exceeds Expectations 5 points	Proficient 4 points	Developed 3 points	Emerging 2 points	Novice 1 point
Content	Includes an interesting and creative, yet simple event that causes the speaker to have a change of mood.	Includes an interesting, yet simple event that causes the speaker to have a change of mood.	Includes a simple event that causes the speaker to have a change of mood.	Includes a simple event, but development of ideas does not indicate the event would cause the speaker to change mood.	Does not follow the format of a simple event causing the speaker to change mood.
Expressive Language	Uses interesting, creative, and engaging language to convey ideas.	Uses interesting and creative language to sufficiently convey ideas.	Attempts to use some expressive language to convey ideas.	Makes minimal attempt to use convey language to express ideas.	Few or no attempts to use expressive language; language used in poem is basic.
Style	Follows rhyme scheme and meter with exceptional use of words and phrases within the poem.	Mostly follows rhyme scheme and meter with interesting words and phrases within the poem.	Somewhat follows rhyme scheme and meter with words and phrases within the poem.	Unable to follow rhyme scheme and meter.	Little or no attempt to follow rhyme scheme and meter.
					_____ / 12

Challenging Common Core Language Arts Lessons: Grade 4 © Prufrock Press Inc.
Permission is granted to photocopy or reproduce this page for single classroom use only.

LESSON 3.2
Metaphor Poetry

Common Core State Standards

- RL.4.1
- RL.4.2
- L.4.5
- L.4.5.a

Materials

- Lesson 3.2 Poem Analysis
- Lesson 3.2 Poem Planning
- Lesson 3.2 Poem Response
- Lesson 3.2 Rubric: Sandburg-Style Poem
- Student copies of "Fog" by Carl Sandburg
- Computer and Internet access

Estimated Time

- 45 minutes

Objectives

In this lesson, students will:
- demonstrate understanding of figurative language by writing a poem using metaphor as a literary device.

Content

Students will create their own poem in the style of Carl Sandburg's "Fog." They will determine the metaphor used in "Fog," choose another type of weather event, and compare it to the attributes of an animal they select as a metaphor for that type of weather.

Prior Knowledge

Students will need to have analyzed the content of the poem "Fog" by Carl Sandburg and the idea of the speaker comparing fog to the behaviors of a cat. Students should know what metaphors are and how to write simple metaphors.

INSTRUCTIONAL SEQUENCE

1. Engage students in a discussion about "Fog" by Carl Sandburg. Discuss the meaning of *metaphor*, and make sure students can see the comparison between the fog and the behavior of the cat. Students can use Lesson 3.2 Poem Analysis to compare the attributes of the cat and the fog. Discuss student responses so that they may articulate their ideas about the comparisons they see.

2. Ask students to consider other natural elements. Have them identify the characteristics of weather events such as wind, rain, snow, or sleet. Create an anchor chart that lists colorful adjectives and verbs associated with them. For example, wind may "howl" or "scream," rain may "pound" on rooftops, thunder "rumbles," or snow may "swirl" and "dance."

3. Next, have students create their own metaphor for a weather event using an animal. Have them refer to the use of the cat in "Fog." Cats are considered mysterious, quiet, and independent animals; the focus is matching the cat and its behavior to the attributes of the fog. Students may have a tendency to choose, for example, a polar bear or walrus to go with a blizzard because of the frequency of blizzards in that animal's habitat, but it may not necessarily be the best choice for a metaphor based on behavior.

Teacher's Note. Consider making an anchor chart of the words and behaviors associated with different animals as was done with the characteristics of weather events.

4. Distribute Lesson 3.2 Poem Planning and Lesson 3.2 Rubric: Sandburg-Style Poem to help students generate a new poem with their ideas.

5. Have students read their completed poems to their classmates. As they are reading, students will complete Lesson 3.2 Poem Response. Once all poems have been read, discuss the poem response chart and any common themes.

Extension Activities

Students may:

- extend their poems by adding more detailed stanzas to further develop how the animal enters, more specific behaviors and actions, and interactions with other animals, plants, people, buildings, etc., to show a more defined understanding of how the natural disasters behave, their effects, and metaphor development; or
- compare and contrast poems written on similar topics but using different animals using a Venn diagram or other comparison chart and write a constructed response on the effect of their animal choices on the overall tone and feel of the poem.

LESSON 3.2
Poem Analysis

Directions: Below are four attributes of cats. Apply the attributes to the four sections of the poem "Fog" to show how the fog behaves like a cat. Some attributes may fit in more than once place, but try and use each attribute at least once. Then, highlight key words in the poem that let you know it is comparing the fog to a cat.

Cats are:
    a. Quiet
    b. Independent
    c. Mysterious
    d. Spend majority of time lying down and sleeping

Lines From "Fog"	Attributes
The fog comes on little cat feet	
It sits looking over harbor and city	
on silent haunches	
and then moves on.	

Nature Versus the Human Spirit

LESSON 3.2
Poem Planning

Directions: First, list four to five attributes of the animal you have chosen that you feel best match the weather event you have chosen. Then, use the attributes to complete the chart with your ideas for your own metaphor poem. Last, highlight any key words that let the reader know you are comparing the weather event to the animal.

Chosen animal: _____

List of attributes:

Weather Event: _____	
Introduce weather	
Introduce animal	
Animal's action or behavior	
Where	
How	
Both the weather and animal exit	

Challenging Common Core Language Arts Lessons: Grade 4 © Prufrock Press Inc.

Nature Versus the Human Spirit

NAME:_____ DATE:_____

LESSON 3.2
Poem Response

Directions: As each classmate reads his or her poem, complete each section. Write the name of the student who is presenting. Name the weather event and the animal. Then write one line from the poem that really gives you a feel for the nature or power of the weather event.

Student's Name	Weather Event	Animal	A Vivid Line From the Poem

Nature Versus the Human Spirit

Student's Name	Weather Event	Animal	A Vivid Line From the Poem

LESSON 3.2 RUBRIC
Sandburg-Style Poem

	Exceeds Expectations 5 points	Proficient 4 points	Developed 3 points	Emerging 2 points	Novice 1-0 points
Poem Structure	Includes all six structural elements: introduce weather, introduce animal, animal's action or behavior, where, how, and how they both exit; poem is creatively and expressively written beyond expectations.	Includes all six structural elements: introduce weather, introduce animal, animal's action or behavior, where, how, and how they both exit.	Includes four or five of the six structural elements: introduce weather, introduce animal, animal's action or behavior, where, how, or how they both exit.	Includes two or three of the six structural elements: introduce weather, introduce animal, animal's action or behavior, where, how, or how they both exit.	Includes one or none of the six structural elements: introduce weather, introduce animal, animal's action or behavior, where, how, or how they both exit.
Quality of Metaphor	Uses vivid words to write about the weather and animal simultaneously; comparison is sharply focused and completely clear.	Writes about weather and animal simultaneously; comparison is clear.	Writes about weather and animal simultaneously; comparison is mostly clear with one or two areas requiring further development.	Attempts to write about weather and animal simultaneously; comparison is somewhat clear with two or three areas requiring further development.	Makes little or no attempt to write about weather and animal simultaneously; comparison is unclear with more than three areas requiring further development.
Characteristics of Weather Event	Includes five interesting weather attributes.	Includes four interesting weather attributes.	Includes three interesting weather attributes.	Includes two interesting weather attributes.	Includes one or no interesting weather attributes.
Characteristics of Animal	Includes five interesting attributes of the animal.	Includes four interesting attributes of the animal.	Includes three interesting attributes of the animal.	Includes two interesting attributes of the animal.	Includes one or no interesting attributes of the animal.
					_____ / 16

Nature Versus the Human Spirit

LESSON 3.3
Opinions on Natural Disasters

Common Core State Standards

- L.4.1
- L.4.3
- W.4.1
- W.4.9
- RI.4.1
- RI.4.9

Materials

- Lesson 3.3 Natural Disaster Research Organizer
- Lesson 3.3 Natural Disaster Prompt Organizer
- Lesson 3.3 Rubric: Opinion Writing
- Student copies of *Hurricanes, Earth's Mightiest Storms* by Patricia Lauber
- Student copies of *Volcanoes* by Seymour Simon
- Writing journals or paper for writing
- Computer and Internet access (optional)

Estimated Time

- 180 minutes (with additional time set aside for research)

Objectives

In this lesson, students will:
- use knowledge gained from reading informational text in order to write an opinion essay on a topic.

Content

Students will choose a topic related to the central idea (e.g., nature is unrelenting, nature is feared, nature affects our daily lives) and write a persuasive essay on the risk involved with living near areas associated with their topic.

Prior Knowledge

Students will need prior experience with writing persuasive essays and the writing process. They should know how to plan and organize ideas for writing. Students should be familiar with the exemplar texts.

INSTRUCTIONAL SEQUENCE

1. After students have read through both anchor texts, engage them in a discussion about the effects of natural disasters on people's lives. Ask: *Should people build homes near places where natural disasters can occur?* Discuss things students should consider (e.g., building codes, resources and technology available, what specific potential losses could occur). Tell students they will be answering this question in a persuasive essay.

2. Distribute Lesson 3.3 Natural Disaster Research Organizer. Students will need to pick a natural disaster to research and complete the chart on the organizer. Allow sufficient time for students to gather and organize ideas. Students may refer to print or online resources to research their topics.

3. Distribute Lesson 3.3. Natural Disaster Prompt Organizer and Lesson 3.3 Rubric: Opinion Writing for students to begin organizing their essays. As students go through the writing process, provide teacher feedback as well as peer feedback. Ensure that students are expressing their own ideas and using the texts as support.

4. Have students type final drafts for submission. Students can also develop a PowerPoint or Prezi to present their main ideas and findings to their classmates.

Extension Activities

Students may:

- use Karen Hesse's *Out of the Dust* to explore the impact of the dust storm on the family by creating a graphic organizer that lists impacts on each character, or by writing an essay on the unrelenting nature of the dust storm and how that affected their livelihood, and the fear that both caused and was caused by the accident with the fire; or

- focus on the following line from "Zlateh the Goat" by Isaac Bashevis Singer: "Aaron did not want to admit the danger, but he knew just the same that if they did not find shelter, they would freeze to death." They may sequence the story from that point, outlining each decision Aaron made out necessity for fear of his safety, and the effect of each decision. Students can then consider Zlateh's role in these events and complete a writing task on how she helped to save Aaron from the unrelenting blizzard.

LESSON 3.3
Natural Disaster Research Organizer

Directions: Select a natural disaster to study and complete the chart below to help answer the research question.

Research Question: Should people build homes near places where natural disasters can occur?

Which natural disaster did you choose? _____

Organizing Question	Research	Source
What does your natural disaster do?		
Where does your natural disaster most often occur?		

Nature Versus the Human Spirit

Organizing Question	Research	Source
What are some ways it can affect people living nearby?		
What are some ways people can avoid the negative effects?		

LESSON 3.3
Natural Disaster Prompt Organizer

Directions: Choose and circle a main idea statement. Fill in your topic on the line.

1. People should build homes near places where _____ can occur.

2. People should **not** build homes near places where _____ can occur.

Fill in your ideas on the chart. Start by giving your own reasons for your opinions. Then, locate one or two pieces of supporting evidence from the text on your chosen topic. Refer back to Lesson 3.3 Natural Disaster Research Organizer as needed. Do not forget to put information into your own words or use quotation marks if you are directly quoting from the text. Use the back of the page for more ideas.

Reason	Supporting Evidence
1.	1. 2.
2.	1. 2.
3.	1. 2.

Challenging Common Core Language Arts Lessons: Grade 4 © Prufrock Press Inc.

Nature Versus the Human Spirit

LESSON 3.3 RUBRIC
Opinion Writing

	Exceeds Expectations 9 points	Proficient 7 points	Developed 5 points	Emerging 3 points	Novice 1 point
Content	Sharply focused on the main idea with ample details provided.	Sufficiently develops the main idea with sufficient details provided.	Mostly develops the main idea with some details provided.	Only some-what develops the main idea with few details provided.	Does not develop the main idea.
Connection of Ideas	Ideas are connected with excellent clarity and critical think-ing is evident; explains whether or not the risks are worth the potential losses.	Ideas are suffi-ciently connected with good flow and clarity; explains whether or not the risks are worth the potential losses.	Ideas are some-times connected with minimal interruption to flow; attempts to explain whether or not the risks are worth the potential losses.	Ideas are not well connected, do not flow well and are difficult to follow; mini-mal attempt to explain whether or not the risks are worth the potential losses.	Ideas are not connected; difficult to read and often does not make sense; no explanation as to whether or not the risks are worth the poten-tial losses.
Evidence	Uses ample, well-chosen evi-dence from text to support main ideas.	Uses sufficient, well-chosen evi-dence from text to support main ideas.	Uses evidence to support some main ideas.	Does not use evidence to support main ideas, or reads as a summary of the text.	Little or no evidence used to support main ideas.
Style	Exemplary com-mand of opinion style that includes use of persua-sive language in interesting and varying sentence patterns.	Sufficient com-mand of opinion style that includes use of persua-sive language in varying sentence patterns.	Adequate command of opinion style that includes some use of persuasive language.	Weak command of opinion style; little use of persuasive language; some-times unclear.	Little or no com-mand of opinion style; very limited or no persuasive language.
Conventions of Writing	No mistakes in grammar, mechanics, or spelling.	One mistake in grammar and/or spelling.	Two or three mis-takes in grammar and/or spelling.	Four or five mis-takes in grammar and/or spelling.	More than five mistakes in grammar and/or spelling.
					_____ / 35

UNIT III

Culminating Essay Prompt

Directions: In this unit, you have examined how nature can change mood, the attributes of weather, and how weather affects people. Imagine that you live in a biome that is weather-controlled. The temperature is always pleasant. You have just enough water to drink and for flora and fauna to survive from a controlled mist, but no more than that. There are no weather events, which means no thunderstorms, no snow, no wind, etc. Using what you have learned about weather, how it behaves, and how it impacts people, write a descriptive or narrative style essay explaining the positive and negative effects the weather-controlled biome would have on the people living inside.

Nature Versus the Human Spirit

UNIT IV

Overcoming Struggles

This unit centers on characters and people who have overcome hardships and become inspirations to others. Within the unit, students will read, analyze, evaluate, and interpret novels and nonfiction texts with themes related to how the characters inspired others through perseverance. They will examine characters and historical figures and identify their individual hardships, their hopes and dreams, and how they handled their roadblocks to success. Students will demonstrate their understanding of this theme through various projects, narrative writing, informational writing, persuasive writing, and poetry.

LESSON 4.1
Interview With a Character

Common Core State Standards

- RL.4.1
- RL.4.2
- RL.4.3
- RL.4.7
- SL.4.3
- SL.4.4

Materials

- Lesson 4.1 Questions for Bud
- Lesson 4.1 Peer Feedback
- Lesson 4.1 Rubric: Interview
- Student copies of *Bud, Not Buddy* by Christopher Paul Curtis

Estimated Time

- 100 minutes

Objectives

In this lesson, students will:
- ask and answer questions using text-based evidence to support choices.

Content

Students will work in pairs as part of an interview scenario. One student will pose as Bud from *Bud, Not Buddy* and another will take on a role as interviewer. Students will determine both the questions they would ask the character about his struggles, causes, and dreams and how Bud would most likely answer those questions, based on his words and actions as presented in the text.

Prior Knowledge

Students will need to have read *Bud, Not Buddy*. Students should be familiar with the different themes and events contributing to the character's development and have an understanding of the different character's traits, motives, and behaviors.

INSTRUCTIONAL SEQUENCE

1. Introduce students to the saying "That which does not kill us makes us stronger." Ask them to discuss this idea and how it relates to *Bud, Not Buddy*. Guide the discussion in the direction of the circumstances that could have kept Bud down, yet he continued on, even when things did not turn out as he had imagined.

Teacher's Note. Consider tying in the struggles that came with being African American in the midst of the Depression, which can easily tie into a social studies unit.

2. Have students work in pairs, with one student in the role of Bud and one as an interviewer. Assign each pair two chapters from the text. Ask students to complete Lesson 4.1 Questions for Bud, which asks them to generate a list of 10 questions they would like to ask Bud about his journey, hardships, dreams, and goals within their assigned chapters.
3. Encourage higher order thinking questions, challenging students to infer Bud's answers and draw from the text-based evidence instead of looking up actual answers straight from the text. Students can use questions that start with how, why, or what if, and pose questions that analyze Bud's thoughts and feelings. They can also use "Do you think/feel" as a springboard. Examples may include:
   - What was going through your mind when you decided to run away?
   - What was going through your mind when you missed the train?
   - Do you think you had luck on your side?
   - What do you see in your future after you receive the horn?

4. Have students work together to devise questions and answers for the interview.
5. As students are working, they should carefully consider how Bud would speak, gesture, and interpret each question being asked. They will need to go back into the text to get clues on his speech and gestures and can draw from events that happened to him to develop his most likely responses to the questions.
6. Have students present their interviews to the class; this need not be a memorized presentation, but more to share ideas and provide opportunities for discussion and feedback. Students should consult Lesson 4.1 Rubric: Interview before presenting. If possible, film the interviews to play back for students. Distribute Lesson 4.1 Peer Feedback form for students to provide feedback to each pair after they have presented.

Extension Activities

Students may:
- write a speech as though they are introducing an adult Bud to a crowd after he has won an award, discussing Bud's life and what he has overcome, as well as making predictions about what might have happened to Bud between the end of the book and receiving the award; or
- complete a "documentary style" interview that encompasses information from several chapters, or even the entire text.

LESSON 4.1
Questions for Bud

Directions: Write 10 questions you would like to ask Bud about his journey, hardships, dreams, and goals, based on the information in your assigned chapters. Focus your questions around the theme, "That which does not kill us only makes us stronger."

Assigned chapters: _____

1.
2.
3.
4.
5.

6.

7.

8.

9.

10.

LESSON 4.1
Peer Feedback

Directions: Complete each part of this form based on the interview being presented.

Presenters: _____

THREE things I liked were . . .

1.

2.

3.

TWO questions I have are . . .

1.

2.

ONE thing I would change is . . .

1.

LESSON 4.1 RUBRIC
Interview

	Exceeds Expectations 5 points	Proficient 4 points	Developed 3 points	Emerging 2 points	Novice 1 point
Theme	Questions clearly relate to the theme selected for the activity and display an exceptional understanding of the theme.	Questions clearly relate to the theme selected for the activity.	Most questions clearly relate to the theme selected for the activity.	Half of the questions clearly relate to the theme selected for the activity.	Few, if any, questions relate to the theme selected for the activity.
Questions	Questions are open-ended and show strong critical and creative thinking, which allow for interesting, thoughtful responses.	Questions are open-ended and allow for interesting, thoughtful responses.	Most questions are open-ended and allow for interesting, thoughtful responses; a few recall or yes/no answers.	Half of the questions are open-ended and allow for interesting, thoughtful responses; half are simple recall or yes/no answers.	Few, if any, questions are open-ended and allow for interesting, thoughtful responses; most questions are simple recall or yes/no answers.
Accuracy of Speech	Bud is portrayed accurately through tone, pitch, volume, and style, with evidence of careful consideration of text evidence to show how his character would speak.	Bud is portrayed accurately through tone, pitch, volume, and style.	Bud is mostly portrayed accurately through tone, pitch, volume, and/or style, or three of the four criteria are identified in the interview.	Attempts made to portray Bud accurately through tone, pitch, volume, or style, or two of the four criteria are identified in the interview.	Little or no attempt to portray Bud accurately through tone, pitch, volume, or style.
Accuracy of Mannerisms	Bud is portrayed accurately through use of mannerisms, gestures, posture, and movement, with evidence of careful consideration of text evidence to show how his character would move.	Bud is portrayed accurately through use of mannerisms, gestures, posture, and movement.	Bud is mostly portrayed accurately through use of mannerisms, gestures, posture, and/or movement, or three of the four criteria are identified in the interview.	Attempts made to portray Bud accurately through use of mannerisms, gestures, posture, or movement, or two of the four criteria are identified in the interview.	Little or no attempt to portray Bud accurately through use of mannerisms, gestures, posture, or movement.

	Exceeds Expectations 5 points	Proficient 4 points	Developed 3 points	Emerging 2 points	Novice 1 point
Evidence From the Text	Responses are clearly linked to the text with accurate, thoughtful answers, student also references other text-based events from earlier in Bud's journey.	Responses are clearly linked to the text with accurate, thoughtful answers.	Most responses are clearly linked to the text with accurate, thoughtful answers, or one or two inaccuracies noted.	Some responses are clearly linked to the text with accurate, thoughtful answers, some responses were general or vague or a few inaccuracies noted.	Responses are general and vague with no clear link to the text.
Originality	Text information is integrated with student's original thoughts and ideas; knowledge of text is applied and synthesized into a thoughtful, original, and creative presentation.	Text information is integrated with student's original thoughts and ideas; knowledge of text is applied and not simply recalled.	Text information is mostly integrated with student's original thoughts and ideas; most knowledge is applied with one or two instances of simple recall from the text.	Text information is not consistently integrated with the student's original thoughts and ideas; most information is taken directly from the text and not applied to the interview.	Interview does not display original ideas and thoughtful design; students are recalling direct quotes from text without application to the task.
					_____ / 24

LESSON 4.2
A Monologue

Common Core State Standards

- RL.4.2
- RI.4.2
- W.4.3
- W.4.9
- SL.4.4

Materials

- Lesson 4.2 Monologue Response
- Lesson 4.2 Monologue Planning
- Lesson 4.2 Rubric: Narrative Writing
- Lesson 4.2 Rubric: Monologue Performance
- Student copies of *Bud, Not Buddy* by Christopher Paul Curtis
- Student copies of *We Are the Ship: The Story of Negro League Baseball* by Kadir Nelson (optional)
- Computer and Internet access (optional)

Estimated Time

- 120 minutes (with additional time set aside for planning)

Objectives

In this lesson, students will:
- draw inferences from information presented in text about a character or person in order to recount an experience effectively.

Content

Drawing from events and information in one of the two exemplar texts, students will deliver a monologue from the point of view of a character chosen from *Bud, Not Buddy* or person chosen from *We Are the Ship: The Story of Negro League Baseball* that explains that person's struggle and dreams for a better future.

Prior Knowledge

Students should be familiar with the content of the exemplar texts. They should have experience with different types of narrative writing (not necessarily monologue writing, but understanding that narrative writing comes in different forms). They should know the parts of the writing process.

Students should be familiar with locating information in texts and drawing conclusions/making inferences about characters or people they read about.

> **Teacher's Note.** Before beginning the lesson, find videos of other students delivering monologues that are available online and choose a couple of appropriate sample monologues for your students to view. Samples are easily found, as monologues are common in theatre, however, a couple of sources include:
> - Monologue Archive (http://www. monologuearchive.com/children.html), and
> - "4 Free Monologues for Kids & Teens" by Beat by Beat Press (http://www.bbbpress. com/2014/07/4-free-monologues-kids-teens).

INSTRUCTIONAL SEQUENCE

1. Ask if any students have prior experience with delivering monologues. Discuss the term *monologue*, and have students read some sample monologues. Have students discuss the monologues and analyze the character, setting clues, point of view, topic, and expressive language used.

2. Distribute Lesson 4.2 Monologue Response. Have students view one or two video samples of monologues and ask them to identify the qualities they observed that made the monologues effective. Engage students in a discussion of their responses, allowing all students to share their ideas.

3. Students should choose a character or person from one of the texts to be the subject of their own monologue. They will write and deliver a monologue as their subject that addresses the character or person's dreams for a better future. Other people or characters can be used that fit into the central idea, as long as information is readily accessible for students to draw ideas from.

4. Set time limits for the monologues (they are typically around 3 minutes in length). Distribute Lesson 4.2 Rubric: Monologue Performance to help students plan.

5. Allow students time to plan for monologues by asking them to locate information in the text that supports how their topic relates to the title, "Dreams for a Better Future."

6. Once students have taken sufficient notes from the texts, the next step is to write the monologue. They should remember that they are going to assume the role of the character and provide his or her thoughts and feelings as related to the topic and speak directly to the audience for the entire time; they will not be interacting with anyone else.

7. Using Lesson 4.2 Monologue Planning, have students begin planning ideas for their monologues. After they have completed the planning page, have students go through the writing process to develop monologues.

8. After final drafts are completed, have students practice their delivery and memorize their monologue (optional). Have students present their monologues, which will be graded using Lesson 4.2 Rubric: Monologue Performance.

Extension Activities

Students may:

- compare and contrast two monologues they have viewed and determine what made one speaker more effective to them, and why (e.g. what could the other speaker have done to have more of an effect?); or
- write a series (3–5) of memoirs, based on the theme "dreams for a better future," as if they were the character from the selected text.

LESSON 4.2
Monologue Response

Directions: While viewing the sample monologue, answer the following questions based on your observations.

Monologue Topic: _____

1. How does the speaker begin the monologue?

2. What was the main idea of the monologue?

3. What helped express the main idea? (Think about voice, tone, gestures, facial expressions, etc.)

4. How does this speaker feel? What clues helped you determine this?

5. What stood out to you the most? Explain why.

6. Do you feel the speaker expressed his or her point effectively? Explain why or why not.

7. How does the speaker conclude the monologue?

LESSON 4.2
Monologue Planning

Directions: Answer the following questions to help you write your monologue.

Monologue Topic: Dreams for a Better Future

1. How will you begin your monologue?

2. How will we know who is speaking, and what the setting is?

3. What is the main idea of the monologue that will support the theme, "Dreams for a Better Future?"

Overcoming Struggles

4. What points will you discuss to express the main idea?

5. What are some powerful words or phrases that will express the main idea?

6. How does the character feel? What nonverbal clues will help others figure this out? (Think about voice, tone, gestures, facial expressions, etc.)

7. How will you conclude your monologue?

LESSON 4.2 RUBRIC
Narrative Writing

	Exceeds Expectations 9 points	Proficient 7 points	Developed 5 points	Emerging 3 points	Novice 1 point
Content	Develops the main idea with ample, well-chosen details.	Develops the main idea with sufficient details.	Mostly develops the main idea with some details.	Only somewhat develops the main idea with minimal details.	Does not develop the main idea; limited or no details.
Development of Ideas	Powerful, creative, and carefully selected words and phrases help develop the character and his thoughts and feelings.	Carefully selected, interesting words and phrases help develop the character and his thoughts and feelings.	Some interesting words and phrases help develop the character and some thoughts and feelings.	Few interesting words and phrases help develop the character and few thoughts and feelings.	No interesting words or phrases help develop the character, limited or no thoughts and feelings.
Evidence	Uses ample, well-chosen evidence from text to support main idea.	Uses sufficient, well-chosen evidence from text to support main idea.	Uses some evidence to support main idea.	Uses evidence that does not support main idea, or reads exactly like the text.	Uses little or no evidence to support main ideas.
Style	Exemplary command of narrative style that includes establishment of character, setting, and situation, with a natural flow; first person point of view.	Sufficient command of narrative style that includes establishment of character, setting, and situation, with a natural flow; first person point of view.	Adequate command of narrative style that includes establishment of character, setting, and situation, with a mostly natural flow; first person point of view.	Weak command of narrative style that includes establishment of character, setting, and situation, with little natural flow; may or may not be in first person.	Little or no command of narrative style that includes establishment of character, setting, and situation, with no natural flow, may or may not be in the first person.
Conventions of Writing	No mistakes in grammar, mechanics, or spelling.	One mistake allowed in grammar and/or spelling.	Two or three mistakes allowed in grammar and/or spelling.	Four or five mistakes allowed in grammar and/or spelling.	More than five mistakes allowed in grammar and/or spelling.
					_____ / 35

Overcoming Struggles

NAME:_____ DATE:_____

LESSON 4.2 RUBRIC
Monologue Performance

	Exceeds Expectations 5 points	Proficient 4 points	Developed 3 points	Emerging 2 points	Novice 1 point
Character and Setting	Character and setting are established and integrated into the performance in a creative and thoughtful manner.	Character and setting are established and integrated into the performance.	Character and setting are established in the performance.	Character or setting is established in the performance.	Character and setting are assumed and not clearly established during the performance.
Character Representation	Character is presented based on a clear and exceptional understanding of character traits.	Character is presented based on a clear understanding of character traits.	Character is presented based on an adequate understanding of character traits.	Character is presented based on some character traits; some flaws present.	Character is misrepresented; little attention paid to character traits.
Gestures and Body Language	Gestures and body language match character traits and actions; are believable, creative, thoughtful, and appropriate to the character.	Gestures and body language match character traits and actions; are believable and appropriate to the character.	Gestures and body language are believable and appropriate for most of the presentation.	Some appropriate gestures and body language are used during the presentation.	Very few gestures or body language are present.
Volume and Tone of Voice	Volume is appropriate, even, and speaker can be clearly heard; tone of voice matches the character representation and gestures with exceptional portrayal.	Volume is appropriate and speaker can be clearly heard; tone of voice matches the character representation and gestures.	Volume is appropriate and speaker can be heard throughout most of the presentation; tone of voice matches the character representation and/or gestures.	Volume is sometimes appropriate and speaker can be heard throughout half of the presentation; some attempt at changing tone to match character representation and/or gestures.	Volume is not appropriate and speaker is often difficult to hear; little attempt at changing tone during presentation.

Overcoming Struggles

	Exceeds Expectations 5 points	Proficient 4 points	Developed 3 points	Emerging 2 points	Novice 1 point
Pace	Pace is appropriate and thoughtful, and the audience is easily able to follow the presentation; pace closely matches character representation and gestures.	Pace is appropriate and the audience is able to follow the presentation; pace matches character representation and gestures.	Pace is mostly appropriate with some unnecessary changes (e.g., too fast or too slow); pace mostly matches character representation and gestures.	Pace is sometimes too fast or too slow for audience to follow; some attempts to appropriately change pace to match character representation or gestures.	Student speaks too fast or too slowly to be understood; little attempt to make appropriate changes to the pace of the presentation.
Focus	Presentation has a sharp focus on the topic with clear link to the theme.	Presentation stays on topic the entire time.	Presentation stays on topic most of the time.	The presentation stays on topic half of the time.	The topic is not clear; the presentation is unfocused.
					_____ / 24

LESSON 4.3
The Movie Poster

Common Core State Standards

- RL.4.2
- RL.4.3
- RL.4.7
- RI.4.2
- RI.4.3

Materials

- Lesson 4.3 Movie Poster Analysis
- Lesson 4.3 Rubric: Movie Poster Project
- Student copies of *Bud, Not Buddy* by Christopher Paul Curtis
- Student copies of *We Are the Ship: The Story of Negro League Baseball* by Kadir Nelson (optional)
- Poster paper
- Computer access (optional)

Estimated Time

- 120 minutes

Objectives

In this lesson, students will:
- create a poster using scenes from a text to support a theme or main idea.

Content

Students will participate in a scenario in which a text is being made into a movie about the main character's struggles to overcome obstacles and achieve their goals. Students will carefully select parts of the text that support the theme and present them in a movie or documentary preview format, ensuring not to reveal too much of the story. Students will create an infographic to serve as the poster for the preview and write to describe the chosen scenes.

Prior Knowledge

Students should have read at least one of the texts, *Bud, Not Buddy* or *We Are the Ship*. Students should understand the themes and be able to select parts of the text that support the theme.

Teacher's Note. You may choose to review and select a few appropriate movie posters that are available online to show the class as a model for their own projects.

INSTRUCTIONAL SEQUENCE

1. Begin by sharing the objective of the lesson with students. Explain that they have been "hired" to create a poster for one of the texts they have read that will be produced as a movie.

2. Show students preselected posters of at least three appropriate movies and advertisements for documentaries that may be more suitable for the nonfiction text. Ask them to identify the elements of the posters that are common to each by completing the lesson 4.3 Movie Poster Analysis.

3. Allow students to choose the text for which they would like to create a poster. Place them in groups according to the text chosen. Distribute Lesson 4.3 Rubric: Movie Poster Project before students begin.

4. Students will create simple drafts of their poster with three chosen scenes from the text that connect to the theme. Students should make careful choices that do not reveal too much of the story, while capturing interesting parts of the text that directly relate to the theme. Stress to students that drafts should be simple, and should not include small details or "perfect" drawings, as students can get too caught up in the details on the drafting process.

5. For each scene chosen, task students with writing a paragraph that explains how the scene connects to the theme using support from the text and why they chose the scene for the poster.

6. Once you have reviewed the drafts of the posters, students may begin on their final drafts on the poster paper. If technology is available, have students draw pictures for the poster and scan the images onto a computer, or take digital pictures of the images and upload them to the computer. Using Canva (https://www.canva.com), students can upload their pictures and place them into one of Canva's poster templates, with options to add text and personalize their designs. The work can be saved and printed for display.

Extension Activities

Students may:
- use the movie poster to write and present a trailer for the movie;
- create a comic book with 5–10 panels that connect to the overall theme of the story, but still tell a complete story; or
- complete Lesson 4.3 Movie Poster Analysis on their classmates' posters to facilitate discussion and allow them to give/receive constructive criticism.

LESSON 4.3
Movie Poster Analysis

Directions: Record your observations about the following aspects of each of the posters you are viewing.

	Poster 1	Poster 2	Poster 3
Colors *What colors are used?*			
Space *How is the space used? Is it cluttered? Is there unused space?*			
Characters *How many characters are shown?*			

Overcoming Struggles

	Poster 1	Poster 2	Poster 3
Other Content *What is on the poster besides characters?*			
Text *What words are on the poster?*			
Other Observations *What other interesting things do you notice?*			

NAME:_____ DATE:_____

LESSON 4.3 RUBRIC
Movie Poster Project

	Exceeds Expectations 5 points	Proficient 4 points	Developed 3 points	Emerging 2 points	Novice 1 point
Title and Author Displayed	Title and author are prominently displayed and integrated creatively into the poster style.	Title and author are prominently displayed and integrated into the poster style.	Title and author are prominently displayed.	Title and author are displayed, but could be more prominent.	Only title or author displayed, or information is not prominent.
Scenes Depicted	More than three interesting scenes are depicted on the poster, poster has a clean appearance and is not too "cluttered."	Three interesting scenes are depicted on the poster.	Two interesting scenes are depicted on the poster.	At least two scenes are depicted on the poster; selection could have been improved.	Only one scene is depicted on the poster, or scenes were not carefully selected/all come from only one part of the text.
Theme Depicted	Each scene has a strong, clear connection to the theme or main idea of the text, the connection is clear from the visual alone.	Each scene has a strong connection to the theme or main idea of the text.	Scenes mostly have a strong connection to the theme or main idea; some explanation needed.	The connection to the theme or main idea is not completely clear; students needed to explain the connection and ideas were lacking in critical thinking.	Scenes show minimal connection to theme or main idea; knowledge of theme/main idea is not strong or completely accurate.
Appropriate Text Details Depicted	Each scene shows appropriate characters and character appearance, correct setting, and a correct character action; tone/mood is obvious in scene selection and color choice; detail choices are creative, unique, and interesting.	Each scene shows appropriate characters and character appearance, correct setting, and a correct character action; attention to tone/mood is also evident in scene selection and color choice.	Scenes show appropriate characters and appearance, correct setting, and character action.	Scenes depict characters, correct setting, and action, with some inaccuracies in appearance, setting, and/or character actions.	Scenes have several inaccuracies in character, setting, or character actions, or scenes only show one or two of the required parts.

Overcoming Struggles

	Exceeds Expectations 5 points	Proficient 4 points	Developed 3 points	Emerging 2 points	Novice 1 point
Poster Appearance	Poster visually reflects a deep understanding of the task and has the appearance of a real-life movie poster; information is neatly and creatively organized, and highly visually appealing.	Poster visually reflects an understanding of the task and has the appearance of a real-life movie poster; information is neatly organized and visually appealing.	Poster visually reflects an understanding of the task and is neatly organized with few suggestions made for improved visual appeal.	Poster is neat and organized, but lacks the visual appeal of a movie poster due to space, lettering, or color.	Student speaks too fast or too slowly to be understood; little attempt to make appropriate changes to the pace of the presentation.
Scene Description	A highly detailed description of the scene, characters involved, setting, and actions, that reflects a deep understanding of the text.	A detailed description of the scene, characters involved, setting, and actions.	A general description of the scene, with the main character involved and actions; may or may not include the setting.	A vague description of the scene that was chosen, without specific references to character names, actions, or other appropriate details.	An incomplete sentence or thought, or incorrect details.
Scenes and Theme	A complete, correct, and thoughtful explanation of how the theme is supported by the scene, with evidence of critical thinking and a deep understanding of the text.	A complete and correct explanation of how the theme is supported by the scene.	A mostly correct explanation of how the theme is supported; additional details may be needed.	A general explanation is provided, but is not strongly tied to the theme.	Explanation is not tied to theme, is incorrect, or includes flaws in details.
Evidence From the Text	The explanation of theme is supported with multiple instances of specific, accurate, and carefully chosen text evidence.	The explanation of theme is supported with more than one instance of specific, accurate text evidence.	The explanation of the theme is supported with one instance of specific, accurate text evidence.	The explanation of the theme is supported with a description of a text event.	The explanation of theme is not supported with correct or accurate text evidence.

	Exceeds Expectations 5 points	Proficient 4 points	Developed 3 points	Emerging 2 points	Novice 1 point
Scene Rationale	Explains a thoughtful reason based on the student's critical thinking about how the scene applied to the activity using carefully selected and expressive language.	Explains a thoughtful reason based on the student's critical thinking about how the scene applied to the activity.	Explains an adequate reason based on some requirements of the project.	Explanation is vague and not closely related to the activity requirements.	Explanation is not related to activity requirements; answers "I liked it" or something similar.
					_____ / 36

Teacher comments:

LESSON 4.4
A Series of Trading Cards

Common Core State Standards

- RL.4.1
- RL.4.3
- RI.4.1
- W.4.2.b

Materials

- Lesson 4.4 Attributes of Trading Cards
- Lesson 4.4 Trading Card Template
- Lesson 4.4 Rubric: Trading Card
- Student copies of *Bud, Not Buddy* by Christopher Paul Curtis
- Student copies of *We Are the Ship: The Story of Negro League Baseball* by Kadir Nelson (optional)
- Computer and Internet access (optional)
- Large unlined index cards and crayons/colored pencils
- Three packages/types of trading cards (sports trading cards work best)

Estimated Time

- 90 minutes

Objectives

In this lesson, students will:
- provide an in-depth description of a character, drawing from specific details in a text.

Content

Students will gather information about the characters and historical figures featured in texts and create a trading card series of "People Who Inspire." They will choose important background information and facts that can be presented on a simple trading card to support the inclusion of these people in the series.

Prior Knowledge

Students should be familiar with the texts being used. Students will need to be familiar with accessing information online.

INSTRUCTIONAL SEQUENCE

1. Begin by presenting the task to students. Tell them that they will be tasked with creating a series of trading cards about "People Who Inspire." Each student will create a minimum of three cards. Show students some sample trading cards, or allow them to share some of their own trading cards if they have them.

2. Ask them to complete Lesson 4.4 Attributes of Trading Cards, which has them examine the attributes of the cards and determine the characteristics they have in common.

3. Discuss what basic components should be included on the trading card, as well as what supporting details from the text they would include that would justify the card belonging to a series of "People Who Inspire." Guide students toward the understanding that they should include how the person reacted or persevered against a challenge, which would help justify that person as an inspiration.

4. Ask students to generate a list of focus questions they should ask in order to obtain the necessary information for the trading card that supports "People Who Inspire." Use only questions that can be answered either directly from the text or through simple research. Keep a list of the questions on the board or on an anchor chart for reference. See the Answer Key at the end of the book for sample questions.

5. Suggest that students may also want to include a relevant quote by the person on their card.

6. Using the exemplar texts, have students select people or characters they think should be a part of this trading card series. Determine if you want to place students into small groups or have them work independently. Allow students to choose three names for their card, or generate a list of names and divide them up amongst the class. Subjects can come from any exemplar text the students have read.

7. Students should start by creating a template either on a large unlined index card, or using computer software. Have them leave space for a picture and a name, and determine where and how to place the information on the front and back. Distribute Lesson 4.4: Trading Card Template and Lesson 4.4 Rubric: Trading Card before students begin.

8. Allow students time to use the focus questions they generated to collect information to include on their trading cards.

9. Next, have students create their trading cards using available supplies and resources.

Teacher's Note. Canva (https://www.canva.com) has some excellent graphic templates that are student friendly. Consider allowing students to choose more people to add to their trading card series outside of the texts read in class as an extension to this lesson. As long as they are able to acquire books or valid websites about the individuals, they may continually add to the series.

10. Display all of the trading cards in the "People Who Inspire" series. Consider inviting other classes to view the series so that your students can present their cards and explain why their subjects were inspirations.

Extension Activities

Students may:

- choose a subject from one of the trading cards and complete an informative writing piece on events in that person's life that helped him or her become an inspiration to others, or
- write a children's picture book on one of their subjects, including basic information about the person, the main events in his or her life, and how/why he or she was an inspiration to others.

LESSON 4.4
Attributes of Trading Cards

Directions: Complete this chart with information about three different trading cards.

	Card 1	Card 2	Card 3
Photo *Describe the card's image.*			
Basic Information *What basic information is given?*			
Detailed Information *What detailed information is given?*			

Overcoming Struggles

	Card 1	Card 2	Card 3
Organization *How is the information organized?*			
Design *What colors are on the card? Does the card have a border or other features?*			
Other Observations *What do you think is the most interesting thing about the card?*			

LESSON 4.4
Trading Card Template

Name: _____	
Dates: _____	Picture
Title/Role: _____	

DID YOU KNOW?

LESSON 4.4 RUBRIC
Trading Card

	Exceeds Expectations 5 points	Proficient 4 points	Developed 3 points	Emerging 2 points	Novice 1 point
Basic Information	Includes person's name, age, occupation, and other basic information, such as spouses, children, hometown, etc.	Includes person's name, age, and occupation.	Includes two of three elements out of name, age, and occupation.	Includes two of three elements out of name, age, and occupation with inaccuracies.	Only includes person's name.
Detailed Information	Clearly and accurately explains important people, events, and obstacles in the person's life, and how he or she overcame obstacles; describes how people respond to this person and what is memorable about them.	Clearly and accurately explains important people, events, and obstacles in the person's life and how he or she overcame obstacles.	Clearly and accurately explains three of the four requirements: important people, events, obstacles in the person's life, and how he or she overcame obstacles.	Clearly and accurately explains two of the four requirements: important people, events, obstacles in the person's life, and how he or she overcame obstacles.	Clearly and accurately explains only one of the four requirements: important people, events, obstacles in the person's life, and how he or she overcame obstacles; or information is unclear and inaccurate.
Justification	Justifies the person as an inspiration to others; connection to the theme is clear; makes reference to whether or not the person was successful in what he or she was trying to achieve.	Justifies the person as an inspiration to others; connection to the theme is clear.	Somewhat justifies the person as an inspiration to others; connection to the theme is somewhat clear but needs more development.	Makes minimal reference to the person as an inspiration to others; connection to the theme may not be clear but an attempt is evident.	Makes no reference to the person as an inspiration to others.
Design	Has an appropriate image; is neat and professional quality; uses appropriate fonts/handwriting and simple, yet polished, design elements.	Has an appropriate image; is neat; uses appropriate fonts/handwriting and simple design elements.	Has three of the four design elements: has an appropriate image, is neat; uses appropriate fonts/handwriting and simple design elements.	Has two of the four design elements: has an appropriate image, is neat, uses appropriate fonts/handwriting, and simple design elements.	Has one or none of the four design elements: has an appropriate image, is neat, uses appropriate fonts/handwriting, and simple design elements.
					_____ / 16

Overcoming Struggles

UNIT IV
Culminating Essay Prompt

Directions: In this unit, you have analyzed characters and their struggles. Using what you have learned about the characters presented, their obstacles, and how they overcame their obstacles, choose one character from *Bud, Not Buddy* and one person from *We Are the Ship* to write an essay comparing and contrasting the two. Key talking points include: What was similar about their obstacles, goals, and dreams, and what was different about them? What was similar or different about the way in which they handled their hardships? How were they inspirational to others? Compare and contrast this information.

ANSWER KEY

Lesson 1.1 Writing Research Questions

Answers will vary, but sample research questions may include:
1. Who invented it?
2. When was it invented?
3. Where was it invented?
4. What does it do?
5. How does it work?
6. What does it look like?
7. How has it changed since first invented?
8. How does it solve a problem/need/issue?
9. How does it benefit people?
10. Was it made on purpose or by accident?
11. Who uses it?
12. What is it used for?

Lesson 1.2 Exhibit Proposal

Answers are in bold.

Invention: Airplanes (Answers will vary depending on the invention.)	
Purpose of Proposal *What are you trying to accomplish?*	**Airplanes belong in a museum of inventions that have impacted lives because they have changed the way we travel, especially to far away places or other countries.**
Brief Description/ Background Information *Who invented it and when, why, and how?*	**Answers will vary, but students should include the inventor, where invented, what they were made for, and how the invention was first designed.**
Justification *How does it fit the purpose of the exhibit series?*	**Answers will vary; students should explain how the invention aids people in their daily life and infer what life would be like without it.**
Exhibit Plan *What will the design include? What objects will be present?*	**Answers will vary.**
Exhibit Diagram *What will your exhibit look like? Draw a diagram.*	**Answers will vary.**

Invention: Airplanes (Answers will vary depending on the invention.)	
Final Statement *Why should your proposal be considered?*	Answers will vary; students can use the sentence structure "I believe [my invention] belongs in the series because [give a summative reason of what makes the invention so important to people]." For example, "I believe airplanes belong in the series because millions of people fly on airplanes every day, all over the world. Getting from one side of the world to another in such a short time would not be possible without airplanes."

Lesson 1.6 Redesign

Answers are in bold.

Facts About My Invention
Students should list three facts about their invention they would like to improve.

How I Would Improve It
Students should provide a reasonable, mostly realistic improvement.

How I Would Justify My Decision
Students should justify their improvement by explaining how it relates to a want, need, or desire in today's world. For example, if studying an airplane, students could write a fact about how many people an airplane can seat, improve it by suggesting more or less seating, and explaining why people today would want this improvement. More seating may help get more people to a popular destination at one time, or less seating may allow planes to be more spacious for a more pleasant trip, or other similar ideas.

Lesson 2.1 Effects of Expansion

Answers are in bold.

Factors	How Was This Problematic?	What Were the Long-Term Effects?
Smallpox	**Native Americans were not immune.**	**Caused emotional and physical scarring, death.**
Animals	**Settlers drove animals away or killed them.**	**Caused lack of food.**
Assimilation	**Native Americans were made to study European religions and English language.**	**Caused loss of identity; Native Americans used their knowledge of English to petition the government over how they were treated.**
Land Negotiations	**Native Americans lost their homes.**	**Caused relocation to reservations.**
Wage Labor	**Native Americans felt they had no choice due to lack of food and loss of land.**	**Many still continue in these industries today (e.g., timber industry).**

Factors	How Was This Problematic?	What Were the Long-Term Effects?
Customs Declared Illegal	**Unable to practice traditions (students can be more specific).**	**Faced consequences and increased risk of traditions dying out.**

Lesson 2.1 Narrative Content Planning

Answers will vary, but a sample response may include:

1. Death of many, any survivors were left with emotional and physical scarring, there was hunger due to animals also becoming ill and being no good to eat.
2. Settlers were killing or running off animals (answers will vary).
3. Where they live, access to birch wood, maple harvest, farming practices, fishing (answers will vary).
4. Answers will vary. Students should select evidence from *The Birchbark House* that explains each item listed in Question 3.

Lesson 2.2 Traditions Maintained

Answers are in bold.

Traditions	How They Were Observed	Evidence of Continuation
Making maple sugar, hunting/gathering/ fur trapping, fishing, teaching young to help others, using birch bark, moving in summer, playing music/dancing, trade, carrying babies, etc.	**Students should cite the evidence of these traditions as seen in the novel.**	**Students may learn that Ojibwe still live on the land, although reduced in size, some still hunt, gather, and make maple sugar to make a living, some Ojibwe have culture centers where they will gather during summers, cultural programs that teach children how to make birch baskets, culture centers also teach the Ojibwe community values.**

Lesson 2.2 Venn Diagram

Answers will vary depending on information on Lesson 2.2 Traditions Maintained, but students should take the information recorded and list the similarities and differences between the Ojibwe of the early centuries to the Ojibwe today. Sometimes information can be both compared and contrasted; for example, Ojibwe still live on the same land, however, it has been vastly reduced and turned into reservations.

Lesson 2.3 Venn Diagrams

Answers will vary depending on which tribe students select, but students should compare the information they learned about the Ojibwe to information from another Native American tribe. Tribes closer to the Ojibwe will likely have more similarities than tribes farther away, as the Ojibwe adapted many traditions of the Plains Indians as Europeans expanded west.

Lesson 2.4 Play Planning

Answers will vary, but a sample response may include:

1. Scene 1: "The Visitor"
   a. Characters: Omakayas, Angeline, Mama, Nokomis, Deydey
   b. Setting: the winter lodge
   c. Tone: sadness, despair
   d. Event: the family slowly starts getting sick, they divide the house between sick and healthy
   e. How Scene 1 supports the theme: The settler was ill with smallpox, which began spreading throughout the tribe.

Lesson 2.4 Script Writing

Answers will vary, but a sample response may include:

1. Scene 1: "The Visitor"
   a. Characters: (1) Omakayas, (2) Angeline, (3) Mama, (4) Nokomis, (5) Deydey
   b. How the scene will start: the family is worried that everyone will become sick, and hopeful that it will pass them over.
   c. Main events during the middle: Angeline gets sick, the house is divided, Mama becomes sick, then Deydey.
   d. How the scene will end: Nokomis and Omakayas are left caring for their family members.
2. Stage Directions: (a) Concerned, confused, following Nokomis around; (b) Spends a lot of time sleeping, looks and acts fearful when awake; (c) Calm voice, body language shows despair, is lethargic when sick; (d) Calm, collected, in control; (e) Quiet, concerned, listens to Nokomis, sleeps when sick.

Lesson 3.2 Poem Analysis

Answers are in bold.

Lines From "Fog"	Attributes
The fog comes on little cat feet	**quiet**
It sits looking over harbor and city	**spend majority of time lying down and sleeping**
on silent haunches	**mysterious or quiet**
and then moves on.	**independent**

Lesson 3.3 Natural Disaster Research Organizer

Answers are in bold.

Organizing Question	Research	Source
What does your natural disaster do?	**Student responses should include a basic definition and a description of how it moves or behaves.**	**Answers will vary.**

Organizing Question	Research	Source
Where does your natural disaster most often occur?	Students should describe where it most often occurs.	Answers will vary.
What are some ways it can affect people living nearby?	Effects on people living nearby could include effects to homes, trees, livestock, food/water supply, electricity, jobs, education, etc. (Students should answer specific to the selected topic.) A few student responses will include positive effects, depending on their topic, such as a flood renewing nutrients in soil or planting new seedlings.	Answers will vary.
What are some ways people can avoid the negative effects?	Student responses should include ways to avoid negative effects, such as construction of homes and businesses, emergency preparedness (e.g. generators, canned goods), buried power lines, emergency alert systems, etc. (Students should answer specific to the selected topic.)	Answers will vary.

Lesson 3.3 Natural Disaster Prompt Organizer

Answers are in bold.

Reason	Supporting Evidence
Reasons given for and against building homes near places where natural disasters can occur should refer to the ways in which people can avoid the negative effects listed on Lesson 3.3 Natural Disaster Research Organizer. Students may also discuss that natural disasters occur all over the world and cannot be avoided. Reasons against building homes near places where natural disasters can occur should refer to the negative effects listed on Lesson 3.3 Natural Disaster Research Organizer.	Answers will vary; evidence from the text should align with the reason presented.

Lesson 4.4 Attributes of Trading Cards

Answers are in bold.

	Card 1	Card 2	Card 3
Photo *Describe the card's image.*	**Answers will vary, but may include responses such as, "full length photo, posed."**	**Answers will vary, but may include responses such as, "full length photo, posed."**	**Answers will vary, but may include responses such as, "full length photo, posed."**
Basic Information *What basic information is given?*	**Answers will vary, but may include responses such as, "name, event, age, hometown."**	**Answers will vary, but may include responses such as, "name, event, age, hometown."**	**Answers will vary, but may include responses such as, "name, event, age, hometown."**
Detailed Information *What detailed information is given?*	**Answers will vary, but may include responses such as, "favorite things, Q&A responses."**	**Answers will vary, but may include responses such as, "favorite things, Q&A responses."**	**Answers will vary, but may include responses such as, "favorite things, Q&A responses."**
Organization *How is the information organized?*	**Answers will vary, but may include responses such as, "2-column list."**	**Answers will vary, but may include responses such as, "2-column list."**	**Answers will vary, but may include responses such as, "2-column list."**
Design *What colors are on the card? Does the card have a border or other features?*	**Answers will vary, but may include responses such as, "purple with gold background."**	**Answers will vary, but may include responses such as, "purple with gold background."**	**Answers will vary, but may include responses such as, "purple with gold background."**
Other Observations *What do you think is the most interesting thing about the card?*	**Answers will vary, but may include responses such as, "the subject is in a traditional gymnastics pose."**	**Answers will vary, but may include responses such as, "the subject is in a traditional gymnastics pose."**	**Answers will vary, but may include responses such as, "the subject is in a traditional gymnastics pose."**

REFERENCES

Baskin, B. H., & Harris, K. H. (1980). *Books for the gifted child.* New York, NY: Bowker.

Center for Gifted Education. (2004). *Exploring nonfiction: Questions and organizers to guide reading and understanding nonfiction texts.* Williamsburg, VA: Author.

Center for Gifted Education. (2011). *Guide to teaching language arts for high-ability students.* Dubuque, IA: Kendall Hunt.

Harvey, S., & Goudvis, A. (2007). *Strategies that work: Teaching comprehension for understanding and engagement.* Portland, ME: Stenhouse.

McKeague, P. M. (2009). *Writing about literature: Step by step.* Dubuque, IA: Kendall Hunt.

National Governors Association Center for Best Practices, & Council of Chief State School Officers. (2010). *Common Core State Standards for English language arts.* Washington, DC: Authors.

Sandling, M., & Chandler, K. L. (2014). *Exploring America in the 1950s.* Waco, TX: Prufrock Press.

ABOUT THE AUTHOR

Lindsay Kasten was raised in Baton Rouge, LA. She attended Louisiana State University, where one of her professors in an instructional methods course saw in her the potential to work with gifted children. She provided the opportunity for Lindsay to complete field experience in a gifted fourth-grade class, and from that moment, Lindsay was hooked. Upon graduating, Lindsay reached out to gifted sites in East Baton Rouge and landed her dream job of teaching gifted fourth graders in 2004. As well as teaching children, she has a great passion for helping other educators through mentorship and presentations. She is currently teaching gifted fourth graders at Parkview Elementary in Baton Rouge. Lindsay is married and has two daughters who both participate in the gifted program in East Baton Rouge schools. Outside of school, she enjoys reading, puzzles, sewing, and cooking. She also enjoys being out and about in Baton Rouge with her husband and children.

COMMON CORE STATE STANDARDS ALIGNMENT

Lesson	Common Core State Standards
Lesson 1.1	W.4.7 Conduct short research projects that build knowledge through investigation of different aspects of a topic.
	W.4.8 Recall relevant information from experiences or gather relevant information from print and digital sources; take notes and categorize information, and provide a list of sources.
	RI.4.1 Refer to details and examples in a text when explaining what the text says explicitly and when drawing inferences from the text.
	RI.4.3 Explain events, procedures, ideas, or concepts in a historical, scientific, or technical text, including what happened and why, based on specific information in the text.
	RI.4.9 Integrate information from two texts on the same topic in order to write or speak about the subject knowledgeably.
Lesson 1.2	RI.4.1 Refer to details and examples in a text when explaining what the text says explicitly and when drawing inferences from the text.
	RI.4.9 Integrate information from two texts on the same topic in order to write or speak about the subject knowledgeably.
	W.4.1b Provide reasons that are supported by facts and details.
	W.4.4 Produce clear and coherent writing in which the development and organization are appropriate to task, purpose, and audience.
	W.4.9 Draw evidence from literary or informational texts to support analysis, reflection, and research.
Lesson 1.3	RI.4.1 Refer to details and examples in a text when explaining what the text says explicitly and when drawing inferences from the text.
	RI.4.3 Explain events, procedures, ideas, or concepts in a historical, scientific, or technical text, including what happened and why, based on specific information in the text.
	RI.4.9 Integrate information from two texts on the same topic in order to write or speak about the subject knowledgeably.

Lesson	Common Core State Standards
Lesson 1.4	RI.4.3 Explain events, procedures, ideas, or concepts in a historical, scientific, or technical text, including what happened and why, based on specific information in the text.
	RI.4.9 Integrate information from two texts on the same topic in order to write or speak about the subject knowledgeably.
	SL.4.3 Identify the reasons and evidence a speaker provides to support particular points.
	SL.4.4 Report on a topic or text, tell a story, or recount an experience in an organized manner, using appropriate facts and relevant, descriptive details to support main ideas or themes; speak clearly at an understandable pace.
Lesson 1.5	RI.4.1 Refer to details and examples in a text when explaining what the text says explicitly and when drawing inferences from the text.
	RI.4.3 Explain events, procedures, ideas, or concepts in a historical, scientific, or technical text, including what happened and why, based on specific information in the text.
	RI.4.9 Integrate information from two texts on the same topic in order to write or speak about the subject knowledgeably.
	W.4.1 Write opinion pieces on topics or texts, supporting a point of view with reasons and information.
	W.4.4 Produce clear and coherent writing in which the development and organization are appropriate to task, purpose, and audience.
	W.4.7 Conduct short research projects that build knowledge through investigation of different aspects of a topic.
	W.4.8 Recall relevant information from experiences or gather relevant information from print and digital sources; take notes and categorize information, and provide a list of sources.
	W.4.9 Draw evidence from literary or informational texts to support analysis, reflection, and research.
Lesson 1.6	RI.4.1 Refer to details and examples in a text when explaining what the text says explicitly and when drawing inferences from the text.
	SL.4.1 Engage effectively in a range of collaborative discussions (one-on-one, in groups, and teacher-led) with diverse partners on grade 4 topics and texts, building on others' ideas and expressing their own clearly.
	SL.4.3 Identify the reasons and evidence a speaker provides to support particular points.

Lesson	Common Core State Standards
Lesson 1.6, *continued*	SL.4.4 Report on a topic or text, tell a story, or recount an experience in an organized manner, using appropriate facts and relevant, descriptive details to support main ideas or themes; speak clearly at an understandable pace.
Lesson 2.1	RL.4.1 Refer to details and examples in a text when explaining what the text says explicitly and when drawing inferences from the text.
	RI.4.1 Refer to details and examples in a text when explaining what the text says explicitly and when drawing inferences from the text.
	RI.4.8 Explain how an author uses reasons and evidence to support particular points in a text.
	W.4.3 Write narratives to develop real or imagined experiences or events using effective technique, descriptive details, and clear event sequences.
Lesson 2.2	RI.4.1 Refer to details and examples in a text when explaining what the text says explicitly and when drawing inferences from the text.
	RI.4.8 Explain how an author uses reasons and evidence to support particular points in a text.
	RI.4.9 Integrate information from two texts on the same topic in order to write or speak about the subject knowledgeably.
	RL.4.1 Refer to details and examples in a text when explaining what the text says explicitly and when drawing inferences from the text.
	RL.4.3 Describe in depth a character, setting, or event in a story or drama, drawing on specific details in the text (e.g., a character's thoughts, words, or actions).
	L.4.3 Use knowledge of language and its conventions when writing, speaking, reading, or listening.
	W.4.7 Conduct short research projects that build knowledge through investigation of different aspects of a topic.
	W.4.8 Recall relevant information from experiences or gather relevant information from print and digital sources; take notes and categorize information, and provide a list of sources.
Lesson 2.3	RL.4.1 Refer to details and examples in a text when explaining what the text says explicitly and when drawing inferences from the text.
	RI.4.1 Refer to details and examples in a text when explaining what the text says explicitly and when drawing inferences from the text.

Lesson	Common Core State Standards
Lesson 2.3, *continued*	RI.4.9 Integrate information from two texts on the same topic in order to write or speak about the subject knowledgeably.
	W.4.7 Conduct short research projects that build knowledge through investigation of different aspects of a topic.
	W.4.9 Draw evidence from literary or informational texts to support analysis, reflection, and research.
	SL.4.1 Engage effectively in a range of collaborative discussions (one-on-one, in groups, and teacher-led) with diverse partners on grade 4 topics and texts, building on others' ideas and expressing their own clearly.
Lesson 2.4	RL.4.1 Refer to details and examples in a text when explaining what the text says explicitly and when drawing inferences from the text.
	RL.4.2 Determine a theme of a story, drama, or poem from details in the text; summarize the text.
	RL.4.3 Describe in depth a character, setting, or event in a story or drama, drawing on specific details in the text (e.g., a character's thoughts, words, or actions).
	RL.4.5 Explain major differences between poems, drama, and prose, and refer to the structural elements of poems (e.g., verse, rhythm, meter) and drama (e.g., casts of characters, settings, descriptions, dialogue, stage directions) when writing or speaking about a text.
	RL.4.7 Make connections between the text of a story or drama and a visual or oral presentation of the text, identifying where each version reflects specific descriptions and directions in the text.
	SL.4.4 Report on a topic or text, tell a story, or recount an experience in an organized manner, using appropriate facts and relevant, descriptive details to support main ideas or themes; speak clearly at an understandable pace.
	SL.4.5 Add audio recordings and visual displays to presentations when appropriate to enhance the development of main ideas or themes.
Lesson 3.1	RL.4.1 Refer to details and examples in a text when explaining what the text says explicitly and when drawing inferences from the text.
	RL.4.2 Determine a theme of a story, drama, or poem from details in the text; summarize the text.
	RL.4.4 Determine the meaning of words and phrases as they are used in a text, including those that allude to significant characters found in mythology (e.g., Herculean).

Lesson	Common Core State Standards
Lesson 3.1, *continued*	RL.4.5 Explain major differences between poems, drama, and prose, and refer to the structural elements of poems (e.g., verse, rhythm, meter) and drama (e.g., casts of characters, settings, descriptions, dialogue, stage directions) when writing or speaking about a text.
Lesson 3.2	RL.4.1 Refer to details and examples in a text when explaining what the text says explicitly and when drawing inferences from the text.
	RL.4.2 Determine a theme of a story, drama, or poem from details in the text; summarize the text.
	L.4.5 Demonstrate understanding of figurative language, word relationships, and nuances in word meanings.
	L.4.5a Explain the meaning of simple similes and metaphors (e.g., as pretty as a picture) in context.
Lesson 3.3	RI.4.1 Refer to details and examples in a text when explaining what the text says explicitly and when drawing inferences from the text.
	RI.4.9 Integrate information from two texts on the same topic in order to write or speak about the subject knowledgeably.
	W.4.1 Write opinion pieces on topics or texts, supporting a point of view with reasons and information.
	W.4.9 Draw evidence from literary or informational texts to support analysis, reflection, and research.
	L.4.1 Demonstrate command of the conventions of standard English grammar and usage when writing or speaking.
	L.4.3 Use knowledge of language and its conventions when writing, speaking, reading, or listening.
Lesson 4.1	RL.4.1 Refer to details and examples in a text when explaining what the text says explicitly and when drawing inferences from the text.
	RL.4.2 Determine a theme of a story, drama, or poem from details in the text; summarize the text.
	RL.4.3 Describe in depth a character, setting, or event in a story or drama, drawing on specific details in the text (e.g., a character's thoughts, words, or actions).
	RL.4.7 Make connections between the text of a story or drama and a visual or oral presentation of the text, identifying where each version reflects specific descriptions and directions in the text.
	SL.4.3 Identify the reasons and evidence a speaker provides to support particular points.

Lesson	Common Core State Standards
Lesson 4.1, *continued*	SL.4.4 Report on a topic or text, tell a story, or recount an experience in an organized manner, using appropriate facts and relevant, descriptive details to support main ideas or themes; speak clearly at an understandable pace.
Lesson 4.2	RL.4.2 Determine a theme of a story, drama, or poem from details in the text; summarize the text.
	RI.4.2 Determine the main idea of a text and explain how it is supported by key details; summarize the text.
	W.4.3 Write narratives to develop real or imagined experiences or events using effective technique, descriptive details, and clear event sequences.
	W.4.9 Draw evidence from literary or informational texts to support analysis, reflection, and research.
	SL.4.4 Report on a topic or text, tell a story, or recount an experience in an organized manner, using appropriate facts and relevant, descriptive details to support main ideas or themes; speak clearly at an understandable pace.
Lesson 4.3	RL.4.2 Determine a theme of a story, drama, or poem from details in the text; summarize the text.
	RL.4.3 Describe in depth a character, setting, or event in a story or drama, drawing on specific details in the text (e.g., a character's thoughts, words, or actions).
	RL.4.7 Make connections between the text of a story or drama and a visual or oral presentation of the text, identifying where each version reflects specific descriptions and directions in the text.
	RI.4.2 Determine the main idea of a text and explain how it is supported by key details; summarize the text.
	RI.4.3 Explain events, procedures, ideas, or concepts in a historical, scientific, or technical text, including what happened and why, based on specific information in the text.
Lesson 4.4	RL.4.1 Refer to details and examples in a text when explaining what the text says explicitly and when drawing inferences from the text.
	RL.4.3 Describe in depth a character, setting, or event in a story or drama, drawing on specific details in the text (e.g., a character's thoughts, words, or actions).
	RI.4.1 Refer to details and examples in a text when explaining what the text says explicitly and when drawing inferences from the text.
	W.4.2b Develop the topic with facts, definitions, concrete details, quotations, or other information and examples related to the topic.